"This book amazed me right away. I have been interested in these themes my whole life and have had an intuitive understanding about what Kendra Jonas is expressing so beautifully, so to have a book articulate it in this way, is a treasure that excites me and relieves me beyond words. As one reads this material, I can confidently say that activations will happen and personal transformation will begin to truly take place. It is saying hello to places within you that have been dormant. It will unlock doorways and let you discover far more of yourself, not just in philosophical terms, but as a grounded being who is expanding in consciousness in the here and now. It simplifies the complex and takes you on a journey into your deepest self. It hands you the lantern and sets you free. This is a brilliant book of spiritual truths that have been lost to us. It gives us permission to set ourselves free and describes what we are made of energetically, which influences this physical experience and guides us home — the home that dwells within. Ascension is very much an inner shift that changes our outer reality and this book will greatly assist one in achieving this."

— Laura Magdalene Eisenhower,
Great-Granddaughter of Dwight David Eisenhower

"Kendra Jonas guides us with grace and ease, on the most important journey of all; *the inner journey* of bringing meaning to our life experience. Transformational at its very core, this book is a must read for anyone on a spiritual path, which should be all of us at this time! *The Link* is no longer missing."

— Mark "Dr. DREAM" Peebler

THE LINK

Connecting To All That Is Through 7 Principles

KENDRA JONAS

The Link Publications
Woodburn, Oregon

Copyright © 2016 by Kendra Jonas
The Link Publications
Woodburn, OR 97071
www.linktothelink.com

Library of Congress Cataloging-in-Publication Data

Printed in the United States of America
ISBN-13: 978-0692598337

ACKNOWLEDGMENTS

For my incredible husband, Rainer: There are no words big enough to thank you for your faith in me, for loving me, and for being by my side through it all. You are my rock and my eternal soul mate. For my 4 beautiful children: Jehremie, Brett, Bryan, and Cameron. I am proud of every one of you. I also want to express gratitude to my Mother, Barbara, Brenda, Rochelle, Sondra, and Sarah, for your continuous encouragement and support. I wouldn't be where I am today without all of you.

TABLE OF CONTENTS

Author's Preface 1

My Story 3

Where I Am Today 19

Introduction 23

CHAPTERS

1: YOU ARE Pure Conscious Energy 25

2: YOU ARE Whole. You Are ONE 57

3: YOU ARE Not The Ego 89

4: YOU ARE Multidimensional 115

5: YOU ARE Timeless, Infinite, and Eternal 145

6: YOU ARE Creative 177

7: YOU ARE Love 207

Questions And Answers 230

Glossary. 235

Sources 237

About The Author 243

AUTHOR'S PREFACE
JOURNEY TO "THE LINK"

In order to write this book, part of my ego had to die. My need for acceptance became inconsequential, because I could not expect you or anyone else to believe or understand all that I went through and how I came upon the principles that were written for this book. No matter how strange or odd, my story needed to be told and this information had to be shared.

I treaded through nearly 25 years of the *unknown* before I realized that my perceived *dark times* were necessary for my soul to be primed for enlightenment. You have undoubtedly experienced your own difficulties and adversities, which is what brought you to this moment and why you are reading this book. You were drawn to this book because you are someone who seeks solutions as opposed to merely focusing on problems. You are someone who asks questions and who understands that when you ask, you will receive. This is the law of the universe. This is why you found this book and why this book found you.

When the old status quo becomes too painful or uncomfortable, we all experience a hunger and a thirst for change. Without the catalyst we call *darkness*, there would be nothing to motivate us; nothing to drive us to ask questions, seek answers, or change anything in our current situation. We would remain too comfortable to venture out and find that something better awaits us.

In my own search to overcome the discomforts of adversity, trauma, and unpleasant outcomes, I discovered there is a common thread that links negativity and positivity together. There is *a link* that binds and unifies all things into one, whether we perceive something as "negative" or "positive".

As I transcribed and wrote about "The 7 Principles of I AM", a shifting began to occur within my consciousness, and I began to see that I had a relationship to *everyone* and *everything* in the universe. Everything had a purpose. Everything was connected and unified, and seeing this with such crystalized transparency is what led to my greatest revelation. In fact, my transformation was so extreme, it did not seem possible that I could grow and evolve this much in a single lifetime. My life was becoming richer. My relationships grew stronger. My health had never been better. Happiness, joy, love, abundance, and peace filled me beyond measure.

Interestingly, my personal successes were minor compared to what I gained within the central core of my being. I was not even trying to achieve any of those things. They were simply the by-products of my transformation. What was happening to me was big — REALLY BIG, and I owed it to the world to share my story, along with "The 7 Principles of I AM" that led to my transformation.

MY STORY

In the fall of 1991, I was enrolled in my junior year at Portland State University. I just became acclimated to attending a University within the heart of a major city when my world suddenly turned upside down.

I had no idea that my education was about to diverge into an entirely new direction, and this was not limited to what I was learning from my college professors at the University. My lessons also did not emanate from any *typical* life experiences. My greatest lessons came out of an expanded awareness of self, which stemmed from going through some of the most frightening, life-altering incidents I could have ever imagined.

October 24, 1991 marks the date when I experienced the first of many extraterrestrial contacts. My first contact was with what people now refer to as *the Greys*. At that time, I had no knowledge of UFO's, extraterrestrials, the Greys, or anything related to this phenomena. Like most people at that time, I had never heard of the 1947 Roswell Crash,[1] the 1961 Betty and Barney Hill Case,[2] or the 1975 Abduction Case of Travis Walton.[3]

As I started digging for information, I found an entire subculture of people were aware of this phenomenon. These people consisted of highly educated researchers, psychologists, physicians, therapists, physicists, award winning journalists, and even whistleblowers who had come forward to share their stories and knowledge with those who were willing to listen. The problem was that most people in mainstream society were too afraid to listen, so this subculture remained underground as a laughing stock of society.

However, about 10 years after my initial contact with the Greys, I began to notice that these beings were starting to make their way into mainstream society, appearing in Hollywood movies, on television programs, on bumper stickers, on t-shirts, and I have even seen the

Greys appear on a few business logos.

The previously held notion that aliens look like the character on the movie "E.T.", or that they look like something out of a horror movie, had been replaced by something more real. To this day, there is still a tremendous amount of skepticism and misunderstanding about who the Greys really are, although mainstream society is starting to become more aware of their existence, at least on some level.

For me, becoming acquainted with the Greys did not happen gently or gradually, because I had no previous knowledge of them when they decided to make their way into my life. They came uninvited; and needless to say, their visits shook my entire world.

On the night of October 24, 1991, a 3-½ foot tall being with a very large head, large almond-shaped black eyes, milky light gray skin, and a spindly body, woke me out of a deep sleep and began to speak to me. He was wearing a white lab coat, like that of a physician or a scientist, but he was not like any doctor or scientist I had ever seen before.

Although he was not moving his mouth to talk, I could hear his voice inside my head without any sound traveling into my ears. I later understood this to be telepathic communication. He talked very fast and seemed to flit around while he spoke, as if he was in a hurry.

During this experience, I could not physically move my body. I was paralyzed, but I wasn't afraid during this first experience. Instead, I was in a state of total shock. I kept trying to comprehend how this strange looking doctor could have possibly entered my room? How did he get into my apartment and who was he?

When he spoke to me telepathically, I noticed he referred to himself as a collective, using pronouns like *"We"* instead of *"I"*, as he explained what he was intending to do with me. There were no other beings in the room other than himself when he said, "This will only take a minute. *We* just need a little skin sample from you. It won't leave a scar any bigger than one of your Chicken Pox scars."

He peered over my head and raised his hand to my face, while holding a small scooping tool. He began scraping an area just a couple of centimeters beneath my left eye. I lay immobilized while he scraped three times and removed several layers of skin.

I screamed, and the sound of my voice echoed inside my head. "Ouch! You're hurting me!"

He heard the thoughts in my head, because he responded telepathically, reassuring me that everything was going to be alright. He didn't react or respond with too much emotion. His tone remained calm and congenial even though I was feeling very upset with him. He hurriedly collected my skin samples into some sort of container, turned around, and walked through my bedroom wall, disappearing into the night.

I lay astonished and told myself I must be dreaming. This can't be happening! How can a stranger that isn't even human enter my bedroom and do this to me? How would a stranger know I had Chicken Pox? Who was this stranger? Whoever he was, I must have imagined all of it, I told myself, and I fell back to sleep.

Upon rising the next morning, I looked in the bathroom mirror and noticed a swollen red area about the size of a dime beneath my left eye where the scraping had occurred. The swollen, red lump was sore and there was a scooped indentation directly beneath it.

I could not deny that what happened was real. The being that took the sample of my skin left physical evidence behind. When combining this with the reality that the intruder was not even human, I began to experience an overwhelming feeling of fear and terror that lingered into the years that followed.

These types of encounters continued for more than 20 years, occurring as often as once or twice a week, and sometimes even more frequently. The visitations were not limited to physical encounters with the Greys, but I was also visited by other strange humanoids who appeared to be more spiritual than physical.

Many visitations occurred in an out-of-body state, in which the spirit part of myself, or *my soul*, was pulled out of my body while sleeping. I would find myself floating directly above my body while I was being communicated with by other worldly beings. I knew these visitations were happening while I was out-of-body, because I could look down and see my sleeping body below.

Although I have never had a near-death experience, having contact or communication with other worldly beings, while having an out-of-body awareness, is synonymous with someone who has had a near-death experience. The out-of-body experiences broadened my awareness of who I am as a being. While many people either "believe in" or "do not believe in" the existence of a soul; for me, it was not simply a matter of belief. I repeatedly had encounters where my conscious awareness existed outside the constraints of my physical body. This involved having regular experiences of flying, floating, moving through solid objects, and having telepathic communication with non-human beings.

I was resistant and very frightened by these experiences, because I did not have the ability to assimilate them into the constructs of physical reality. I dreaded when the next visit might come, and had trouble going to sleep at night. I would set my alarm at certain times to try to wake myself up randomly in an attempt to disrupt the visitations. I would call out for help during the out-of-body retrievals. I would pray, and I tried using my own willpower to make it all go away, but nothing worked.

My sense of stability, safety, and trust in the world was quickly diminishing and the visitors didn't seem to care or realize how their visits were terrifying me. They continued on with the visits, and as much as I didn't want anything to do with alien visitations, they kept proving their existence was very real.

My fiancé, who was living with me at the time, had some parallel experiences along side mine. Sometimes we would have the same dream or we would see the same UFO appearing in our dreams, and other times these strange occurrences made their way into our physical environment.

Paranormal activity started to occur in our apartment such as the television turning on and off by itself on several occasions. We also witnessed a plastic lid float out of our kitchen cupboard, sailing about five feet across the room and then slam onto the floor, defying all laws of gravity. Sometimes a gust of wind blew through the apartment, causing the door between the bathroom and the bedroom to slam shut. Yet, there was no draft coming from anywhere, nor were there any doors or windows opened that could have caused the wind. We heard and saw unusual sounds and objects that could not be explained, and we frequently had the feeling that we were being watched or followed.

Although some of these unexplained occurrences were shared, the majority of the nighttime visits continued to happen to me alone. I began to feel more and more isolated and helpless. My free will had been taken away and my sense of reality had been completely turned upside down and replaced by the unknown.

In 1996, I began to experience panic attacks. The episodes of panic grew so frequent and severe that it didn't matter whether I was at home, at work, at the grocery store, or visiting with friends or family. I started experiencing dozens of panic attacks every day. It became increasingly difficult to leave the house without feeling overwhelmed and anxious. The panic continued to worsen as the days turned into weeks and the weeks turned into many long months.

I decided to make an appointment to see a Psychiatric Nurse Practitioner who not only diagnosed me with severe Panic Disorder, but also PTSD (Post Traumatic Stress Disorder). My therapist was perplexed by the degree of PTSD I was experiencing. She compared it to that of someone who had trauma from a war or from having repeated occurrences of severe sexual or physical abuse.

I wanted to hide under a rock when my therapist asked the next question, "What happened that could have led to these diagnoses?"

I was not a veteran of war, nor did I have a history of severe physical abuse, sexual abuse, or trauma. My *secret life* was now staring me in the face, ready to seep out into the open, exposing me to a level of vulnerability that I wasn't sure I could bear. I could not expect my therapist or anyone else to believe me or empathize with what I was going through, when they themselves were not going through similar experiences. I feared that if I told anyone about my experiences, they would think I was insane.

I needed to tell her the truth, so I bit my lip and began sharing bits and pieces about my extraterrestrial visitations. Although she was not familiar with the alien abduction phenomenon, she kept an open mind and began exploring this possibility through her own research. After a few more appointments, my therapist concluded that in her professional opinion, I did not have Schizophrenia nor was I delusional. I had simply undergone some type of severe trauma that was most likely due to the nature of the abductions themselves.

Even though the root cause of my anxiety, depression, and PTSD was not well understood, I was relieved to know that upon sharing some of my experiences with a mental health professional, I was not labeled as insane, nor was there any indication that I was going crazy. I had to find answers and make sense out of what was happening to me. The loneliness was unsettling and this drove me to find other people who were going through similar experiences. As alone as I felt, I knew deep down that I couldn't be the only person on the planet who was having nighttime visits with aliens.

I located a support group called The Portland UFO Group (PUFOG), which met once a month in my local town. While attending one of those meetings, I was put in touch with a researcher named Barbara, who was knowledgeable on the subject of UFO's and extraterrestrials.

Barbara interviewed many people who had similar experiences to what I was going through; some of whose experiences became publicly documented cases.[4] I was nervous, but I made an appointment with her.

During our meeting, I told Barbara about my experiences and was relieved that she did not think I was some sort of kook. In fact, the moment I met her, I felt I knew her from somewhere before, but could not put my finger on where or how I knew her. Interestingly, she had this same feeling about me, so we shared information with one another about our past places of employment, places we lived, where we grew up, and who we were associated with to try to find the connection or understand the uncanny feeling that we had met each other somewhere before.

That night, my wonder about how I knew Barbara was answered. During the middle of the night, I had a visitation from a Grey extraterrestrial who took me back into another lifetime when I lived as a Native American woman. I discovered that Barbara was a man at that time and she was my husband. Prior to this, I was not a firm believer in past lives, but this all changed after I had the extraterrestrial-facilitated, past life regression.

During this experience, it was as though I stepped into another body, in a completely different time, but I was still me. I relived several memories, as I went through scene after scene, re-experiencing the past, which felt all too familiar. I noticed through my surroundings, the clothes I wore, and the way my family members spoke, that I was revisiting a time and a place from a very long time ago.

The Grey continued to expose me to other past life memories and said, "The people in your life today have been with you in other lives before."

I felt like a time traveler. With the Grey's guidance, I left my present consciousness once again and was shown a panorama of more past lives. I continued to be taken further back in time until I encountered a life I lived four lifetimes ago. With each life I was shown, I dwelled in a different body, played different roles, and dealt with various life circumstances that pertained to that particular environment.

I saw an unfolding, which was the metamorphosis of my soul, as I explored the continuum of lives I lived. With each consecutive life, my soul was evolving to be more loving, more whole, more wise, and more connected to oneness. I recognized several significant people from my past lives that made their reappearance in the lives that followed. Today, I consider these people to be members of my soul group.

A soul group is an emotionally close group of people who normally incarnate together. Soul groups often experience multiple lives with one another, sharing one common goal, which is to live out various roles so they can help each other grow and ascend spiritually. Some members of our soul group do not incarnate, but instead serve as guides in the spirit realm. For those who *do* incarnate with us, we may share several life experiences with the same members of our soul group, again and again. Becoming aware of our past lives or recognizing people in our soul group can help us see the broader picture.

As I approached my thirtieth birthday, I was receiving fewer visits from the Greys. Instead, the majority of my visits were from some other type of interdimensional being. These other beings sometimes took on a physical form and other times they appeared shadowlike.

When they did take on a physical, human-like form, their skin was bumpy, wart-like and scaly, and they were brownish, green, or olive in color. These beings also had a very large head and large almond-shaped eyes like the Greys, but these were not the Greys.

I knew I was being visited by another type of extraterrestrial, but why? Why was this continuing to happen to me? Was it not enough to deal with being exposed to one type of extraterrestrial, but now, I was being exposed to several? And what's worse was the beings that continued to visit me didn't offer any explanations about *why* they were visiting me. I needed to find other people who were having similar experiences. I needed some answers.

While searching the Internet, I discovered that these interdimensional beings, like the Greys, had a name. People were referring to them as *the Reptilians*.

The Reptilians are known to have olive colored skin that is bumpy or wart-like when they express themselves physically. They have also been called *Shapeshifters*, because they are considered interdimensional and have the ability to change shape or become invisible as they move in and out of the visible spectrum.

They are able to transform from being in an energetic state to having more of a solid form. Because of the many peculiarities associated with these types of beings, I found my experiences with the Reptilians to be even more frightening than what I had experienced with the Greys.

In a typical encounter, I would be asleep, but would suddenly wake up to my entire body feeling like it had a 'pins and needles' sensation. I would find that I was completely paralyzed and unable to move.

In the midst of feeling overcome with fear and terror, a being would say to me, "Do not be afraid. This will only take a minute. We need to adjust your torsion field." Other times I was told, "We need to make an adjustment in your frequency."

In addition to hearing the being speak to me, I would see an alien presence or I would see a shadowlike figure appearing next to me in the room. Even though my physical body was paralyzed, and I could not open my eyes or speak, my soul slipped out of my body, always hovering slightly above. I was able to observe everything with this other part of my conscious awareness.

What followed were waves of electricity *or some type of energetic current* entering my body from the top of my head that surged down into my legs. When this happened, I would usually receive about 5 to 10 blasts of this energy that surged through me so fiercely I could see flashes of white light pulsate under my eyelids from the pressure. Rhythmic swooshing sounds whirled inside my ears. There was no pain associated with these types of experiences.

Only the sensation of energy moving through my body, and of course there was always fear.

One night after crawling into bed, I was feeling very frightened and confused over everything that was happening and I still had no solid answers as to "why" all of this continued to happen, so I cried out for help. I didn't know who I thought would hear me, but I remember how desperate I felt when I asked for help.

Suddenly, I heard a female voice telepathically answer my plea. I was not paralyzed. I was not dreaming. I was fully awake. I had never heard a voice speak to me, that first did not wake me up from a deep sleep and paralyze me. There was no one in the bedroom but me.

The voice said, "It's okay. I am here now and I can help you. I am your guide and I am here to assist you while you continue your life here on this earthly plane. You can rely on me anytime you need. Anytime you have a question or feel scared. I am here."

"Who is this? What is your name?" I asked.

"I reside in the fifth dimension. We don't have names in the fifth dimension. The identification with names is how you operate in the third dimension. What would you like to call me?" She replied.

"You do not have names in the fifth dimension?" I was puzzled.

The voice continued, "We are a collective group of beings who have been called upon to help humanity. We share a unified consciousness but we also have a separate consciousness. Beings in the fifth dimension are telepathic, so we don't rely on names to identify ourselves. Names are constructs applied to third dimensional reality."

Over the next several days, I spent time communicating telepathically with this being. I found I could easily contact her anytime I wanted, so I asked a lot of questions. I received answers to many things I wondered about for a very long time, and for the first time, I felt like I was building *a reciprocal* relationship with a higher dimensional being.

This was unlike anything I had ever experienced, and it was a welcome change compared to all the abduction experiences. This being looked after me and my family's health and wellbeing. She diagnosed my youngest son with Gluten Intolerance before any of the doctors knew what was wrong. I discovered she was quite a healer and she taught me how to naturally heal both my emotional and physical body from various ailments. My mysterious rashes quickly went away. I no longer had any more symptoms of Fibromyalgia. I was no longer catching the common cold. I required less sleep, had more energy, and was growing healthier compared to any other time in my life.

I decided to name my guide "Melody", because of the peace and harmony she was bringing into my life. Talking with her was reassuring and pleasant, and her expression of unconditional love was amazing.

I felt comfortable asking Melody questions and one of my questions was, "Why have I been experiencing visits by strange beings that paralyze me and blast me with some type of energy?"

She answered, "To understand this from your third dimensional perspective, you were originally a fifth dimensional being, before you incarnated on this earthly plane. Part of your soul, from your higher self in the fifth dimension, branched off so you could incarnate in physical form, on earth, with the intention of aiding and assisting humanity. Many souls from the fifth dimension made this choice. However, many of you got stuck here for thousands of years, in what you might call a karma trap. This happened because in order to incarnate in a flesh body, your vibration and your DNA changed and adjusted to inhabit such a body. In doing so, you had forgotten about your fifth dimensional existence. Although fifth dimensional consciousness is still connected to you, because you are always connected to your higher self, it has taken you a long time to realize this. It has taken many lifetimes, as a matter of fact."

She continued, "In order for your third dimensional consciousness to finally reconnect to your higher self in the fifth dimension, we have had to gradually manipulate and adjust your frequency and your DNA while you are living on this earthly plane. The Grey extraterrestrials assisted in the genetic alterations with your DNA. A specific type of Reptilian, who always had your best interest at heart, assisted in adjusting the energetic components of your being, which is why you experienced the electrical energetic charges from time to time. Therefore, both the Greys and the Reptilians provided the necessary alterations to help you reconnect with your fifth dimensional consciousness."

She added, "None of us in the fifth dimension would have been able to reach you in your third dimensional state of existence had these alterations not been made. Gradual manipulations occurred over a period of time, so that your vibrational frequency would be a match to ours in the fifth dimension. This was necessary so we could help you remember what you originally came here to do."

The words, *"what I originally came here to do,"* echoed through my mind, resonating a level of truth. Ever since I was a child, I felt a relentless feeling, a nagging, that there was something I must do. This feeling was unsettling and uncomfortable at times, but I knew if I kept my eyes, ears, and mind opened, I would eventually figure out what this *something* is. *"What I originally came here to do,"* was finally revealed to me, when I was met by *another* fifth dimensional being.

This new being introduced himself by appearing in my dreams almost every night for several weeks. One night, in the middle of my dream, I woke up. To my surprise, the being who I was just dreaming about continued to speak to me telepathically. I knew this was not an ordinary dream. I was having contact once again.

Similar to Melody, this being told me that he does not identify himself with a name, so I decided to call him "Baariq", which is a Muslim name meaning "shining, illuminating, and bright."

Baariq worked with me every night for about 2 months. I never saw that he had any form or a body. I could sense his presence, his energy, and the sound of his voice was very distinct. He was highly intelligent, energetic, loving, and always positive. He communicated telepathically, and the sound of his voice carried the most amazing tone that rang of unconditional love and wisdom. There was resonance in every word he spoke, and every word penetrated the depths of my soul, and filled me with so much wisdom.

Baariq taught me how we create reality with our thoughts and emotions, and that our physical experiences serve as mirrors, reflecting our own perceptions back to us. He showed me the multidimensional nature of the universe and that we ourselves are multidimensional. I learned how to work with other people interdimensionally to help them heal physically and emotionally. I began to see and experience reality as energy that can be manipulated. Everything he came to teach me began to bleed into my physical reality in the way of synchronicities. I was led to videos and articles following the contact experiences with Baariq, which further supported everything he was teaching me.

Baariq's transmissions came at any hour of the night, so I kept my cell phone next to my bed and used my digital notepad to record the transmissions. He deliberately slowed his speech whenever I transcribed his messages into my phone's notepad, so I could keep pace with everything he said. I typed his words exactly as I heard them.

He said, "You are a multidimensional being. You are just not yet aware of your multidimensional nature. Your higher self dwells here with us in the fifth dimension while another part of you resides in the third dimension. As a being in the fifth dimension, your job is like that of a Librarian."

He continued, "You have the ability to tap into and retrieve information directly from a universal database that links to the source for all of creation. Your unique talent is in the way that you decode and translate information into a form we can all understand. You have the ability to give creation itself, a voice, and you do this in a way, unlike anyone else."

He paused as if to allow me time to absorb this information. "You must come to understand how to use this gift in the wisest way. It can be abused. It can be taken for granted. It can be misunderstood. Knowing this is your gift and it is the job that your higher self does in the fifth dimension does not mean that you are going to have all the answers, but you are able to translate the most difficult to understand concepts in the most profound ways. You are thereby a channel for creation and not for any specific entity. An aspect of your soul has chosen to incarnate on planet Earth at this time, which is what you would say, is an aspect of your future self, from your perspective. In reality, your fifth dimensional self and the 'self' you are experiencing on planet Earth right now, exist simultaneously. Linear time does not actually exist at all. It only exists from your third dimensional perspective. All aspects of one's self, (past, present, and future probabilities) can be accessed at any time when the right conditions are met."

A few nights after that transmission, I woke up again to the sound of Baariq's voice. He came to introduce me to my higher, fifth dimensional self and asked if I was ready to merge with her? I was afraid of the thought of merging with anything or anyone, even if this was with another version of myself.

What could this possibly mean? Would I lose my identity or become possessed? I was afraid of this request for a merging, because the idea that we are multidimensional beings and that parts of the "self" can merge together to create a more unified, whole person was completely foreign to me.

After briefly thinking this through, I knew I needed to let go of my fear and allow my higher self to fully integrate into my third dimensional body. From what I was told, I had reached a point in my own spiritual ascension and vibration where this merging was now possible, but it was up to me to agree to the merge.

I made the decision in agreement, and in that instant, the merge happened. From that moment forward, I began to feel physically different. I felt more grounded and more solid in my physical body. I instantly felt more confident in sharing my truth, and I no longer felt ashamed about my unusual experiences. I did develop bouts of vertigo, however, which were frightening. I was told not to worry about this. It was due to the assimilation of higher frequencies within a lower density body.

Fifth dimensional consciousness was now at my disposal and I could access higher levels of consciousness, infinite wisdom, and heightened intuition anytime I wanted. I knew it was time to come forward and share everything that was being revealed to me.

WHERE I AM TODAY

The merge with my higher self did not change my personality. I am still the same person residing in the third dimension with the same history, life circumstances, and physical appearance that I've always had. What has changed is I have become more whole and complete within myself. I have accessed a new frame of reference where I can access information from somewhere else.

This information first comes into my mind in the way of condensed downloads, and then moves into my heart where it becomes processed, felt, and understood. From there, I shape the information into my own spoken or written words. Other times, words are spoken directly to me. I have received information this way from Melody, Baariq, and from an androgynous, loving voice that I call, "The Voice of Creation".

One evening, while I was in the early stages of writing this book, I was feeling very frustrated. I had the passionate desire to write, because insightful information was constantly streaming to me, but I didn't have any idea where my book was headed. I printed out all my notes and spread the loose pages across my floor. I struggled to put ideas into categories with hopes to find structure, but nothing made sense. Overwhelmed and exhausted, I crawled into bed and told the universe that I was ready to give up.

Later that night I awoke around 3:00am to "The Voice of Creation". As usual, this voice did not identify itself with a gender, name, or any kind of label. I recognized this voice by the way it spoke; softly, swiftly, fluently, and with great clarity about the message it wanted to get across. There has never been any confusion or misunderstanding when I hear this voice, because the words hold a concise and powerful vibration.

This telepathic voice spoke powerfully, yet gently, and said, "It is time to wake up now, because you will want to write this down."

I blinked a few times and rubbed my eyes. I reached for the notepad on my cell phone and began typing everything the voice said.

"There are seven principles of I AM. Your book is going to be about these seven principles. It will be revealed that I AM consciousness is not separate, external, or something that is only found in God or within an external being. *Every living thing* holds the same capabilities, wisdom, and knowledge within itself, and this is an exact replication of the creator. YOU ARE the I AM."

The seven principles were then spoken to me in totality, without any hesitation. I typed them exactly as I heard them:

1. I AM Pure Conscious Energy
2. I AM Whole. I AM ONE
3. I AM Not The Ego
4. I AM Multidimensional
5. I AM Timeless, Infinite, and Eternal
6. I AM Creative
7. I AM Love

After I received the seven principles, The Voice of Creation continued, "These will be the seven chapters in your book. The next time you look at your notes, you will know exactly how this all fits together."

The rest is history, because the next morning, I could clearly see how all the pieces fit together. I suddenly had a book. Yet, the night before, all I had was a bunch of random notes.

After that night, The Voice of Creation continued to make brief interjections every time I started a new chapter. I found this was to introduce the concept of that particular principle within those first few paragraphs.

I italicized the information from The Voice of Creation and signed the transcriptions in this way. It was up to me to expand upon the information beyond what was given, by sharing my own experiences, finding research to back up the seven principles, and it was up to me to turn these difficult concepts into something we can all understand.

I accredit this book to be a collaboration from The Voice of Creation, the fifth dimensional guides, Melody and Baariq, who facilitated the merging with my higher self, as well as the hard work that comes from having a third dimensional existence. It was this collaboration that brought this book into existence.

As a transmitter for "The 7 Principles of I AM", I experienced its transformational effects while writing this book. I began to uncover answers to questions I had been asking my whole life. I have a strong sense that this book will affect you in similar ways.

There is a restless feeling inside every one of us that whispers, "There must be something more, something better, and something that is within our grasp, if only we could be shown what this *'something'* is or where to find it." This feeling is a real yearning.

We all experience this because we have dormant DNA that some scientists refer to as "junk DNA". This means that we already contain the blueprint to be able to access an even greater expression of ourselves. Our dormant DNA is just waiting to be unlocked and realized.

The seven chapters in this book present, "The 7 Principles of I AM", and this may be the key to unlocking dormant DNA that will ignite the ascension process in all of us. There is an invisible thread that connects us to one another and to everything in the universe. We are already connected to a higher consciousness that some have referred to as the quantum vibrational field, the higher self, the morphogenic field, or the source field. Our ability to access this field through "The Link" has always been there, but when we live in fear, it becomes veiled and hidden from our awareness.

Once we come face-to-face with fear and turn fear into positive energy and positive experiences, then "The Link" will be rediscovered, connecting us to a greater, cosmic mind. What once seemed *impossible* becomes *I'm possible*.

This has not been an easy journey for me, but as the writer of "The Link", I have been shown that we are much more than what we have been led to believe. The greatest expression of who we are, as part of the collective human race, is about to be exposed and realized. The information contained in this book provides a gentle nudging, to help you remember who you are as a human soul, why you are here, and that a better future is imminent, because no matter what path you are on, every path will eventually lead towards ascension. This book simply serves as a gateway to access certain tools, to help you remember what you may have forgotten along the way. With the light of awareness turned on, we no longer need to fumble around in the dark.

INTRODUCTION

What was once thought to be superhuman, impossible, or that which could only be characteristic of a deity, God, or Gods, are actual aspects of human consciousness. These powerful aspects of your true self have been lying dormant within you, just waiting to be realized. The only reason you have been blocked from experiencing yourself in this way is because you first have to know these things exist within you so they can be expressed through you.

You have not been told the truth about all that you are, all that you are made of, and all that you are capable of. You have not been told that YOU ARE "The 7 Principles of I AM", because these truths have been hidden from human consciousness, until now.

"The 7 Principles of I AM" will show you all the ways that your true self is much greater and more powerful than you once thought. "The Link" has been written to bring forth a deeper understanding about the nature of human consciousness so you can learn how to realize self empowerment, experience more abundance, feel more love, achieve greater wisdom, and experience more peace and harmony in your life.

This book will not change you. This book will honor you, just the way you are, by uncovering aspects of yourself that are begging for reconnection. As hidden layers of your core self become exposed and discovered, this awareness alone will bring more greatness into your human experience. You will come to know yourself as a powerful being that has a co-creative relationship with the entire universe.

There is a link that connects us all to a greater consciousness, but when we adhere to a belief system that is representative of separatism, lack, disconnection, and limitation, instead of one that is representative of unity, abundance, connection, and infinite possibilities, then "The Link" will be veiled from our awareness. "The Link" never disappears and is never out of reach – but because of the paradigm we have been living under, as defined by the constructs of duality, most of us have been unaware that we can tap into an infinite source of energy to manifest more of what we want, any time we want.

This vibrational field of energy links all things together. It is the energy field that exists as *All That Is*. Once you know this and how to tap into this field, and when you know that you are not separate from it, you will no longer feel like a puppet that is being pulled by the strings of life. Instead, you will know all the ways that you are the puppet master. You are the one pulling the strings, accessing infinite wisdom, abundance, and higher consciousness, because you are linked to a field of oneness.

When reading the beginning of each chapter, as transcribed from The Voice of Creation, think about this voice as one that can come in many forms. It is the same voice that resides within you — that reveals resonance, knowledge, and truth.

This greater wisdom and awareness can come to you through various life experiences, through dreams, through creative inspirations, or through any number of ways. There are an unlimited number of ways that The Voice of Creation expresses itself, communicates to you, and works through you.

It is the message that is important and not *who* or *what* the messenger is, because if we focus on *labeling* the messenger, we will lose the deeper meaning and wisdom that is contained therein. I welcome you to join me on this transformational journey while we explore this greater wisdom contained within "The 7 Principles of I AM" that YOU ARE.

CHAPTER ONE

YOU ARE PURE CONSCIOUS ENERGY

Dear One,

You have been led to believe that you are only a physical being and that your entire self is contained within a physical body. Your body is not your SELF. Your SELF is your consciousness and it exists outside the constraints of time and space. Your body is simply a vehicle or a container, allowing you to experience a physical existence so that you can receive, transmit, transform, and co-create energy, because your consciousness is comprised of energy. This means that YOU, as a being of energy, can never be contained, confined, or destroyed. You are infinite and eternal.

Your true self is the "I AM" presence that exists in you, outside of you, and around you simultaneously. You are ONE with this energy, because your consciousness and core existence is actually formless and energetic. Knowing that you are a beacon of formless energy means that you are malleable and capable of becoming all you can create yourself to be in any moment. You are as free as your imagination will take you and you are as abundant as you decide you want to be. As you continue to discover your true energetic nature and your creative potential, you will begin to see that your consciousness is expansive and you are evolving within the body of creation and not separate from it. There is no aloneness or separateness within the energetic field of creation, because everything is always linked to this one vibration.

Energy is abundant and never runs out, because it is linked to All That Is. You are part of this greater energy field that continues to expand out infinitely, branching out into unlimited probabilities and possibilities. This is your energy. This is you. Moving through you, around you, encapsulating you into physical form while maintaining your core existence, which is formless. You are pure conscious energy.

Transcribed From:
The Voice of Creation

. . . .

"The day science begins to study non-physical phenomena, it will make more progress in one decade than in all the previous centuries of its existence. To understand the true nature of the universe, one must think in terms of energy, frequency and vibration." – *Nicola Tesla*

"Energy cannot be created or destroyed, it can only be changed from one form to another." – *Albert Einstein*

The universe is an ocean of energy and we are all part of it. From the subatomic level, to the most complex of creation – everything is pure energy.

Although energy cannot be seen, it can be felt and experienced in many ways. For example, before the invention of satellite transmission, we relied on *rabbit ears* or antenna to receive radio and television signals. Whenever one stood next to an antenna, the signal would improve. No physical contact was necessary in order for the picture on the TV screen to become clearer or the static on the radio to disappear. The human body and the energetic component surrounding the body, known as the aura, are both capable of receiving and transmitting energy.

What we perceive as our *physical world* is actually not as solid as it seems. When examining the ratio of physical matter compared to empty space, we find that physical matter is only a miniscule component of the universe. The majority of the universe consists of empty space, and that which we call space, is actually an endless sea of vibrating energy: Seventy three percent of the universe is made of dark energy, twenty three percent of the universe is comprised of a similar dark matter, while only four percent is *normal matter* that we can see and feel.[5]

When examining this four percent we call matter, whether we are looking at planetary bodies and asteroids, or looking at the atoms within our own bodies, we find that at the subatomic level, the ratio of an atom is comprised of 99.99999 percent energy and only 00001 percent material.[6] If we live in a universe that has been scientifically proven to be made of mostly energy, then why does everything we see and touch appear to be physical and solid?

When quantum physicists studied atomic and subatomic particles at the smallest scale, they discovered that physical reality is not what it appeared. In 1801, Thomas Young conducted the first Double Slit Experiment. This experiment was repeated numerous times, only to discover the same strange results: When scientists fired electrons, (tiny bits of matter), or photons, (tiny particles of light), through a screen with two slits, something unexpected happened. Scientists found that electrons and photons took every possible path and behaved as if they were waves of probabilities any time they were not observed. However, whenever there was a conscious observer, the waves behaved differently and collapsed down to one point as a particle.[7] According to this scientific breakthrough, our consciousness and our ability to perceive, is what creates our perception of physical reality.

This Double Slit Experiment stunned the greatest scientists of all time, including Einstein who said, "Reality is merely an illusion, albeit a very persistent one." In spite of what science has shown us for over 100 years, we continue to discredit what this says about human consciousness and all that we are capable of. We are more comfortable with the belief that physical reality defines us, rather than acknowledge that our consciousness defines our reality. "The Link" was written to help unify science and spirit into one complete understanding so we can integrate what has been proven scientifically into our everyday lives.

According to the Double Slit Experiment, the ability to perceive is what turns raw energy into matter so it can be experienced as physicality. Everything is pure energy until a conscious connection is made. Energy then transforms into something more as soon as it is observed or perceived.

As an example, we can consider the way this book was written and how it transmits information. If your consciousness was not participating in reading this book, then this book would appear to be nothing more than stacks of paper bound together with black inked letters scattered throughout the pages. This book, as well as everything in your physical environment only has *the energetic potential* to carry information. The act of reading this book allows you, the conscious observer, to magically turn paper, ink, and binding material into something more. This is the way your consciousness operates in the universe, turning energetic probabilities into something it can experience, and this is done through the simple act of observation.

No two people will perceive or be affected by information in the same way, yet the words in this book do not change. How can the same sets of words be perceived in so many different ways?

The answer is consciousness. Every individual's consciousness experiences vibrations of energy in its own unique way. You are constantly transforming, transmitting, and recreating energy into something more. You are a co-creator of creation itself. Even though every person reading this book will perceive the information a bit differently, you will get the information you need as though this book was written just for you. The reality is, this book was written just for you, because the printed text cannot become something more until your consciousness participates in the affect it has on you.

When we raise our awareness and begin to view ourselves as energetic beings, instead of merely physical beings, then the science begins to make sense. The definition of how we describe "reality" changes, because as co-creators or active participants in our experiences, physical expression becomes more about internal perception. We begin to see how our own consciousness can and does influence physical reality. We are spiritual beings made up of energy. Our third dimensional, physical existence is the by-product of the way we manifest and work with energy.

You Are A Conduit For The Transmission And Transformation Of Energy

Your body is a vessel for expressing energy. You are emitting energy in everything you interpret, feel, do, and say. When you are doing what you love, living life to the fullest, or doing what you call your *life's passion*, you are expressing your highest energetic vibration, which is love. You are made of love and you are a co-creator of love. Love is the highest energetic frequency that exists within us and without us. It is the blueprint for All That Is. When you operate from the standpoint of love, you are in alignment with the vibration of life itself. Love is synonymous with creation, and vibrating from this state is what brings about your desired manifestations.

Artists, scientists, musicians, and inventors, who live a life of passion, often claim they don't know where their ideas come from, how their artwork takes shape, or how sound comes through as a series of harmonious tones, becoming music to our ears. Those we know as incredibly talented people or prodigies are tapping into an external field of expansive creative energy. This energy comes through their *crown chakra* in the form of ideas and inspiration.

The inventor, writer, artist, or musician then moves this energetic vibration into the heart. From there, it becomes channeled and expressed as emotional energy for others to experience. Their experience is described as timeless and non-material. The music, art, or the words, come *through* them and not *from* them. When they step aside and realize what they have created, they are just as mystified by the magic as those who witness their talents. We all have the ability to tap into this energetic field of love and express it in our own unique ways, simply by following our inspiration and our heart's desire.

Manifestation Is The Transmission Of Energy From The Imaginative Mind To The Heart

Everything that has ever been invented, created, built, or achieved, started out as a *thought*. An artist creates art out of seeing and perceiving something that inspires him or her. The word "inspired" is taken from the idea that with every breath, we are infused by spirit. Creative energy moves through us with every breath, and we become *inspired* or *in-spirited*, which means to be filled with or guided by spirit.

Even though the act of creating begins in the mind, it also involves the heart. It is not *what* the artist sees that is reflected in the art, but it is *how* the artist sees, which manifests when energy moves from the imagination to the heart. The act of creating and manifesting is the collaboration between the mind and the heart. In reality, we are all artists, creating, manifesting and painting our reality all the time, whether we are consciously aware of this or not.

Emotions are comprised of the same energy as thoughts, but this energy transforms when it moves from our *mind-space* into our *heart-space*. The word "emotion" (e-motion) actually means *energy in motion*, which is experienced through the act of *expressing* one's feelings. We all have the ability to *express* our feelings, and when we do this, we are actually channeling emotional energy outward, just as we have the ability to hold back our feelings and trap energy in our body.

When we contemplate the words we use in our language, we are reminded of the ways we work with energy all the time. Energy moves through us and we are constantly working with energy even when we are unaware of this. Moving and manipulating energy from our thoughts, to our emotions, to our actions, is how we co-create and manifest everything into physical reality.

When you visualize something in your mind and combine this with passionate emotional intention, you are moving energy from your mind into your heart. Your heart is the gateway to your *sixth sense*, which is linked to universal consciousness. YOU ARE a receiver, transmitter, transformer, and co-creator of energy. The essence of who you are is not only comprised of energy, but you also transmit energy, because you are capable of imagining, perceiving, feeling, and expressing your intentions. Your mind is your receiver and your heart is the engine that converts energy into motion, giving thoughts their power to take form. Your *free will* and desire to take action ignites your intentions, which creates manifestations.

Your Sixth Sense – The Missing Link

The ancients referred to intuitive thought as the *sixth sense*. The Eye of Horus (originally, The Eye of Ra) is an ancient Egyptian symbol of protection and power. The eye consists of six separate parts that come together to create the illustration, representing all six senses (Fig – 1).[8] The corresponding parts of the eye and the six senses are: Smell, Sight, Thought, Hearing, Taste, and Touch.

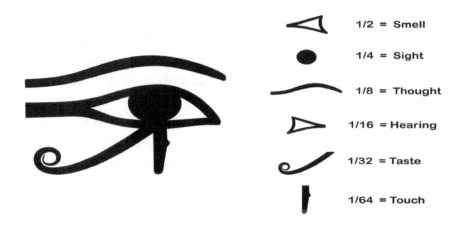

1/2	= Smell
1/4	= Sight
1/8	= Thought
1/16	= Hearing
1/32	= Taste
1/64	= Touch

(Figure – 1)

The idea of having six senses was reduced to only five senses by Western Science, so the sixth sense of *thought or intuition* was removed from being recognized as a sense, and no one seems to know why. What if the ancients knew something about *thought* that we have yet to figure out? Perhaps something significant about *thought* has been deliberately swept from our awareness, to prevent us from realizing our greatest potential. Perhaps our *sense of thought* is what links us to an energetic field that exists throughout the universe. The way we receive thoughts and inspirations may be similar to the way our computer connects to the Internet.

The brain's neurons transmit electrical signals through an internal delivery process, but neurons might also *receive* information from a larger cosmic mind; capturing, receiving and processing external data called *thoughts* into *thought-forms*, which we identify as our own. If thoughts originate from a larger cosmic mind, then there is nothing mysterious about acknowledging that we have a sixth sense. Just as photons of light or sound waves provide us with the stimulus that gives rise to seeing and hearing, it is possible that an external, energetic stimulus gives rise to our ability to experience thought. In other words, we can *experience thought*, but we do not *create thought* any more than we create the air that we breathe. We choose the types of thoughts we invite into our mind and decide which thoughts we will give attention to. Once we understand what the ancient's knew about the sixth sense of thought, we can strive to connect to a greater, cosmic mind, where we can link to expanded ways of thinking.

In our language, we speak of the way thoughts enter or pop into our mind. Thoughts must originate from somewhere, because everything comes from something, so how does a thought enter into the mind in the first place? We *perceive* and *experience* thoughts hundreds of times each day, but are we really the original creators of thought? These next several pages reveal how thoughts, ideas, and consciousness are not actually dependent on the physical brain at all.

Electrical Activity In Space Could Be *The Link* To A Larger Universal Brain

The image on the left (Fig-2)[9] is from a photograph taken in 2010 from the Chandra, Hubble, and Spitzer's high-powered telescopes. This image is a computer simulation to illustrate the distribution of dark matter in the universe. These images resulted after taking photos in space using the world's most advanced digital cameras. The image on the right is a photograph of nerve cells in the brain. (Fig-3) [10]

   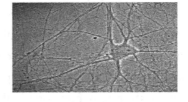

(Figure - 2)   (Figure – 3)

What was once thought of as dark, empty space appears to be

something that looks electrical in nature, and looks very much like the inner workings of the brain. If we knew that imaginative, creative, and intuitive thought came from a greater cosmic mind, we could learn how to tap into this field more deliberately and expand our creative potential. We could find better solutions to everyday problems, discover new inventions in an instant, create breathtaking art and beautiful music, and the list goes on.

Talented prodigies, musicians, artists, and inventors may already be doing this. This would explain where genius comes from, how inspirations are conceived, and why the physical brain does not have to operate optimally in order for genius to occur.

If the physical brain operates like a computer, it would make sense that "something" *could* plug into it, similar to the way a computer connects to the Internet. When your computer or your brain is offline, it operates from its own programs, internal intelligence, and wiring. Likened to a computer connecting to the Internet, we may be able to link to higher levels of thought through our sixth sense, which links us to a universal mind, extending far beyond that which is contained within the walls of the physical brain.

There are individuals with brain injuries who have difficulties with basic cognitive tasks, such as talking, writing, and tying their shoes, yet, they can play Mozart the first time they hear it. There are documented cases of people with autism who cannot calculate basic math concepts, but can tell you the day of the week that a particular date falls on at any point in time.[11] There are cases of people who have had an accident that resulted in severe brain trauma, and upon recovery, they are suddenly able to play a musical instrument without any previous experience, or speak fluently in another language they had no previous exposure to.[12][13]

Another strange occurrence is that the greatest inventors in history came up with the same inventions around the same time. For example, Calculus, The Theory of Evolution, The Polio Vaccine,

Einstein's E=mc2, and even the telephone all had simultaneous inventors working on these same inventions at the same time.[14] It appears as though *something external* is inspiring multiple people to create or invent the same things at the same time. Odds are very slim that simultaneous inventions occurring at the same time could all be just random coincidences.

What we consider "genius" is not something derived from the processes of the physical brain, but rather those that exhibit "genius abilities" are tapping into something much greater, outside of themselves. This can be likened to *a cosmic Internet.*

Inventors, artists, musicians, and savants are tapping into a greater mind outside of themselves. This provides the most plausible explanation as to why ideas for inventions have been accessed simultaneously, and why works of art, music, and mathematical formulas have come from people who did not even have to *think* about what they were doing. People are *downloading* ideas for their art, music, and inventions, externally, from a mind outside of their physical brain, because all of this has been known to occur even when there is evidence of brain injury, brain trauma, and when the brain is not working optimally. In fact, it has been shown that when cognitive processes are suppressed, or when we enter into an altered state of consciousness, an expanded super-intelligence is unleashed, linking us to our divinity.

Consciousness And Telepathy

As an energetic being, your consciousness exists beyond that which is physical. Studies of telepathy, out-of-body experiences, and near-death experiences, demonstrate that thought and consciousness are not confined and experienced merely inside the brain. We will look at several studies to demonstrate how thought and consciousness have been proven to exist outside of the physical brain, including studies of Extrasensory Perception (ESP) and telepathy.

Dr. Rupert Sheldrake, Ph.D. biologist, researcher, and author, demonstrated that telepathy; precognition, extra sensory perception, and intuition are natural aspects of thought. Based on hundreds of studies replicated by several scientists, Dr. Sheldrake concluded that the mind extends beyond the walls of the skull and functions similar to the way cell phones emit a frequency. Just as there is a magnetic field around the earth, there is energy that extends outside of the brain, which he refers to as the "extended mind".[15]

Most of us have had the feeling of knowing who is calling on the phone before we answer it. The person who is about to call you suddenly appears in your mind and then you realize you were just thinking of that person prior to receiving their call. Some scientists dismiss these common occurrences as coincidences, not worth studying. However, when this phenomenon is studied, it is discovered that the results are far from being coincidental.

In one of Dr. Sheldrake's studies, participants provided four phone numbers of close friends or family members. The friends or family members were randomly selected to call the participant and the participant was asked to guess who would be calling before the call was placed. There should have only been a 25 percent chance that the participants would guess correctly, however the actual percentage of the participants who guessed correctly was 45 percent. These results did not change when the callers resided in a distant country, but the emotional closeness between the caller and the participant did play a factor. The results were the most accurate when the caller felt emotionally close to the person being called, while acquaintances or unfamiliar callers had the lowest hit rate.[15]

Telepathic phenomenon is not only common with humans, but there is plenty of evidence to show that telepathy is common between pets and their owners too. Studies have been done with dogs, cats, and even exotic birds, and the results show that pets and their human companions commonly share telepathic experiences.

Nearly 50 percent of dogs anticipate their owner's arrival for home. For this study, Dr. Sheldrake placed video cameras in the dogs' homes and the dogs were observed when the owners were not there. When analyzing the videos of dogs in their natural home environment, it was noted that the dogs began to wait by the door or window to anticipate their owner's arrival whenever the owner started to leave for home or had *the thought* or *intention* of wanting to leave for home.[15]

All routines and patterns were changed, so this ruled out the possibility that the dogs were behaving from a conditioned response. The modes of transportation changed, the distance traveled varied, and the times for each departure changed, which eliminated any variables. It was apparent through video observation that the act of *thinking* about leaving for home, or starting to leave for the destination of home was what caused the greatest response in the dogs' behavior.[15]

We have all experienced times when it seems like someone has read our mind or we have sensed strong emotions coming from another person, even when words were not spoken. Most of us have had the experience of sensing a stranger staring at us from a distance, only to turn around and suddenly lock eyes with the other individual. We have all experienced various degrees of intuition. Nonetheless, we rarely question the mystery about *why* these occurrences happen, so we write them off as coincidences. However, for scientists who have studied the phenomenon of ESP, they have provided enough evidence to demonstrate that these are not coincidences. Something more is going on with human consciousness that cannot be explained by the operations of the physical brain.

Your Consciousness Persists Beyond Space, Time And Even Death

You are always a conscious observer, observing your experience from various perspectives. Whether you are awake, asleep, or in a dream-like state, you are still the same observer in your experience. What is most interesting is that consciousness has been proven to exist without a brain and without a body. Numerous documented cases of near-death experiences provide validation for this, which we will examine next.

A bestselling book was made into a motion picture called, "Heaven is for Real: A Little Boy's Astounding Story of His Trip to Heaven and Back", by Todd Burpo and Lynn Vincent.[16]

This book is based on a true story about a four-year-old boy named Colton who had a near-death experience during emergency surgery. He reported being able to look down and see the doctors operating on him while his dad prayed for him to survive. The boy met his sister during his near-death experience, but prior to this, he never knew he had a sister, because she had been miscarried and no one told him about her. He also met and accurately described his great grandfather who died 30 years before Colton was born.[16]

Hundreds of reports of near-death experiences were examined and researched by Dr. Bruce Greyson M.D., an author of several articles and a book he co-authored called, "Irreducible Mind: Toward a Psychology for the 21st Century." Dr. Greyson delivered numerous presentations about his findings, enlightening many scientific communities and neuroscientists about the true nature of consciousness.[17]

In one of his presentations titled, "Is Consciousness Produced By The Brain?", Dr. Greyson described credible evidence and case studies about people who experienced conscious awareness when medically, this should have been impossible.[17] Even when patients were pronounced clinically dead or suffered severe brain injuries, these patients provided credible proof that they still experienced consciousness. Nearly one thousand patients studied had critically impaired brain function through severe head trauma, or they were revived after being pronounced dead. In every case, the patients were able to report specific events that took place in the hospital or operating room even though their brain was not functioning at the time.[17]

In one example, a man who was near-death underwent coronary bypass surgery. After he was anesthetized, he reportedly had an out-of-body experience and observed his body lying on the operating table, while he hovered from the ceiling above. He noticed one of the surgeons appeared to be flapping his arms as if he had wings and was trying to fly.

The day after the operation, the patient asked the doctor why he was flapping his arms so oddly during the surgery? The doctor explained, rather embarrassed, that he communicated this way to the operating nurses and surgeons because he had on sterile gloves. To prevent any cross contamination, he placed his hands against his chest to avoid touching any surfaces and he used his elbows to point, gesture, and direct the other surgeons throughout the operation.[17]

The details witnessed by the patient during his operation were so specific that the patient had to be conscious in order to accurately comment on the doctor's behaviors and mannerisms; yet the patient was unconscious and his vital signs were declining. Additionally, he reported the incident from the perspective of one who was looking down from the ceiling instead of from the perspective of lying on the operating table.

In another case, a boy with meningitis had a near-death experience in a hospital after having a severely high fever for more than 36 hours. The attending physicians did not believe the child was going to survive and his parents remained by his bedside day and night. Miraculously, the boy recovered and reported back to his parents that he had died and went to heaven, and while he was there, he spoke with his older sister, who was attending a University at the time, and she told him to go back.[17]

His parents were disturbed by their son's story or they assumed he was hallucinating from having had a high fever. They called the University where their daughter was attending, and to their devastation, they discovered their daughter had been killed the night before in an automobile accident. No one in the family had been notified of her death until the next day when her parents called to check on her.[17] Consciousness continues to exist, not only in the location or room where the individual is having the near-death experience, but individuals who are near-death also report having contact in other realms, or describe having communication with loved ones who have already deceased.

In addition to near-death studies, Dr. Greyson researched children all over the world who recalled detailed events of having past lives. In these cases, children's recognition was so vivid that they were able to remember specific names of people, occupations, locations, and detailed accounts from past lives, which resulted in reuniting with living family members and friends they left behind from their previous lives.[17]

If consciousness existed in the brain, it would not continue to exist once the brain dies. Yet, consciousness has been proven to exist in every case, even when there is no physical capacity for it to do so. For generations, there have been thousands of documented cases of near-death experiences and past life memories reported by people all over the world.

The understanding that consciousness does not need a brain can also be seen in plant studies. Plants do not have a brain, and yet, it has been shown that a form of consciousness exists in plants.

Cleve Backster, founded the C.I.A's polygraph program. In 1966,

Backster decided to connect his polygraph machine to a houseplant. "In human subjects, a polygraph (or lie detector) measures three things: pulse, respiration rate, and galvanic skin response, otherwise known as perspiration."[18]

Backster was curious to see if a houseplant would respond to the polygraph test, so he thought he would light a match and set one of the plant's leaves on fire. To his surprise, before he even pulled out the match, the polygraph registered an intense reaction. Not only did the houseplant demonstrate a reaction in the polygraph, but it also appeared to read his mind.[18]

Since that time, Backster and other independent researchers have conducted similar experiments with vegetables, fruits, bacteria, algae, eggs, and human cell samples. They found that individual cells also responded electrochemically to the donor's emotional states, even when the donor was not in the same room, building, or when the donor resided in another part of the country.[18]

Consciousness Is Connected By A Network Of Unseen Energy

We can conclude from Backster's polygraph studies of plants, that consciousness resides in all living things. Not only that, but conscious beings are able to sense and respond to one another in the absence of a brain or a physical body. There wasn't any physical contact made when Backster intended to light a match to burn one of the plant's leaves. Yet, the plant was able to sense energetically that there was the *intent* to harm. Dr. Sheldrake demonstrated that sensing and responding to intention, which we call ESP, occurs not only among people, but this has also been observed between people and their pets.

The interconnecting nature of consciousness can be explained using the analogy that there is *an invisible link* that connects everything to a larger grid or network, similar to the way your computer connects to the Internet. This explains why telepathic communication and ESP do not have a preference, whether this is human-to-human telepathy, human to animal telepathy, or plant to human telepathy. We are all connected to an unseen field of energy.

We are energetic beings. We can exist without a brain. We can exist without our senses. We can exist in the absence of a physical body. This means that we are also infinite, because energy can never be destroyed. The energetic components of your consciousness may change, but *you* will always exist, as the one perceiving all of your experiences.

Your Chakras Are The Body's Energy Portals

Although we cannot see or experience all forms of energy, energy is moving through us constantly. For more than four thousand years, ancient cultures all over the world have adhered to the concept that "portals" exist within the body, which serve as a bridge between the cosmic life force energy and the body's organs.

The common thread of ancient knowledge has *linked* our ancestors to the same truth, even though they did not have contact with one another as a form of influence.

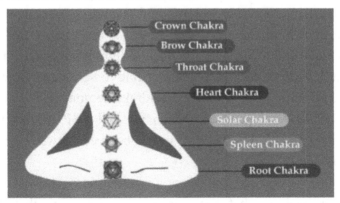

(Figure – 4)

These vortices or vortexes, otherwise known as chakras, are doorways that operate a bit like sponges, providing us with the ability to receive, transmit, store, and work with life force energy.

Each chakra is said to be a "force center" or a receptor for the transmission of energy. Chakras work with both physical and spiritual energy, because chakras link the two realms together, transforming the spiritual into physical, and the physical into spiritual.

Tangible things, like the food we eat and the environment we live in, as well as intangible things like thoughts and emotions, all have a direct influence on our chakras. The chakra's portals draw energy from Prana, which is the Sanskrit word for the life force energy.[19]

When this energy is pulled through the chakras, it becomes transformed into various vibrations, which we need for our physical existence. The Hindu chakra system acknowledges that there are seven main chakras or portals in the body.[20]

Chakra #1 – Your Muladhara Or Root Chakra

Your "Muladhara" Root Chakra is the first chakra located at the base of the spine. This chakra responds to all things physical. The Root Chakra is connected to all the other chakras, even though the Root Chakra is the lowest chakra and it is furthest away from the seventh chakra, or the Crown Chakra, which is that of divine spiritual awareness and fulfillment.

When you take action physically, whether this is through yoga, exercise, physical labor, or expressing yourself sexually, you are triggering this life force energy to move through your Root Chakra. Negative energy that's been stored in the body from the stressors of daily living are released, replaced, and renewed when the life force energy moves through this chakra. This is why all of these types of physical activities are considered stress relievers.

If your Root Chakra is underactive, you may experience fatigue, anxiousness, or nervousness. To resolve an imbalance in your Root Chakra, simply find ways to engage your physical body so you will become more grounded. You can do this by doing something active such as taking a walk or raking leaves. You can also direct energy to the Root Chakra by doing this meditation exercise:

> Stand barefoot outside so your feet are in direct contact with the soil or the grass. As you stand, imagine a cord starting at the top of your head that penetrates down through your core and comes out between your legs, grounding you to the earth as if you are a tree with powerful roots that hold you to the ground. When you do this simple meditation, you will instantly have the sensation of being more physically grounded. You will begin to notice your legs will get heavy and you will become more focused on being in your physical body.

Positive Feelings Of Safety & Security Improve The Energetic Flow To The Root Chakra

It is important to feel safe, secure, and confident in your dealings with money, relationships, and in your home life. Only *you* have the power to drive your emotions, so if you have a belief that expresses lack because you believe your environment does not meet your survival needs, then it is important to either change your environment, or change your *attitude* about your environment.

For example, if you believe that you can live comfortably on less money every month, you will select a lifestyle in your environment to match this belief. You will find the right combination of resources that will allow you to live comfortably on less, such as by having roommates or shared housing, taking public transportation, using government resources, or cutting back on other things, so that your environment matches your beliefs about living frugally.

Likewise, if you believe you cannot feel financially secure until you find a different job or receive a pay raise, then it's important to pursue whatever you need to do so your physical environment matches your beliefs. The only way to feel safe and secure with your current situation is to either change the belief about how you define your sense of safety and security, or you will need to change your environment to match your beliefs. Either way, it is the *belief about finances* that determine one's sense of financial security and not the financial situation itself.

Feeling safe and secure is an internal state of being that is not actually related to external affairs. If we feel unsafe and insecure, it is because *we believe* that something in the external world is dangerous, harmful, and affecting our well-being. Events and circumstances are only threatening if we perceive them in this way.

When we are stressed, worried about the future, or have regrets from the past, we block the life force energy from moving through our chakras' portals. Negative emotions block and restrict the flow of energy, which will eventually lead to illness and disease. Our thoughts have a direct impact on our emotions, and since our emotions are energetic, this is what brings forth physical manifestations – both positive and negative.

Chakra #2 - The Swadhisthana Or Sacral Chakra

The Swadhisthana Chakra is located approximately 3-5 inches below the navel and is associated with empathy, emotional sensitivity, and creativity. Balancing the feminine and masculine energies within ourselves will allow the life force energy to move through this chakra.

Most of us have been taught to repress certain emotions that we believe will cause us to appear weak, or we are afraid to allow ourselves to be who we truly are through our own unique self expression. Allow your gentle nature to come out, by expressing tenderness, sensitivity, and compassion for yourself and others. You can give yourself permission to feel vulnerable by embracing any flaws and imperfections within yourself. Shamelessly loving everything you have ever done, said, or experienced, without judging yourself will bring more life force energy to this chakra. Likewise, feeling judgmental, resentful, angry, unworthy, guilty, or repressing heartfelt emotions will block the energetic flow to this chakra.

This chakra is the gateway to the inner child. Children freely express their emotions and creativity without judging themselves or others. To maintain a healthy energetic flow through this chakra, it is recommended that you allow yourself opportunities to play like a child.

Give yourself time each day to recreate, which literally means to re-create, explore, seek new adventures, relax, and have fun. Allowing time for recreation is not only relaxing, but it is necessary for your mental, emotional, and physical well-being.

Chakra #3 - The Manipura, Solar Plexus Chakra

Have you ever had a sinking feeling in the pit of your stomach, or had a "gut feeling" when something made you feel uneasy? When you feel nervous, do you experience the sensation of butterflies in your stomach? Likewise, when you feel enthusiastic, do you notice the sensation of joy and excitement dancing in your stomach?

The life force energy is always with us, but depending on what you believe to be true about your abilities, determines how this energy will be expressed. For example, the sensation of butterflies in the stomach before you go to a job interview, take a college midterm, or give a presentation, occurs from a lack of confidence in your abilities. However, once you change your beliefs about what you are capable of, your emotions will radiate a higher vibration, and the feeling of butterflies in the stomach will convert to excitement and enthusiasm.

Depending on what thoughts you have, the life force energy will transform to match the same frequency that is reflective of your thoughts and beliefs. If you are confident, you will feel excited in your core. If you are fearful, you will experience this life force energy as an unsettled feeling, which is always felt in the pit of the stomach, through this third chakra.

To channel this energy positively and experience it as a zest for life or as unstoppable confidence, simply change your thoughts and beliefs about yourself. Believe you are a winner who is capable of success in whatever you do.

Confidence is nothing more than believing you can do something instead of thinking you can't. When you allow yourself to feel confident about anything, your anxieties will dissolve, and fear will convert into passion. Otherwise, having negative thoughts about yourself can lead to chronic anxiety disorder, stomach ulcers, and other digestive illnesses, because you are literally blocking this life force energy from doing what it was designed to do – which is to fill you with over-flowing passionate excitement.

Chakra #4 – The Anahata, Heart Chakra

Similar to the way your physical heart pumps blood throughout your circulatory system, your Heart Chakra also operates like an engine, pumping and transmitting energy out into the universe through the power of your emotions and intentions. We experience emotions or (e-motions), energy in motion, in the form of feelings.

Your emotional energy can either be directed out into the universe away from the body, or it can remain inside the body where emotions can become trapped, depending on whether you "express" your feelings or keep them inside. Your Heart Chakra is responsible for manifestation and fueling the laws of attraction, because your heart has a built-in relationship with a larger cosmic mind. When your Heart Chakra is balanced, you will feel connected to those around you, to nature, and to All That Is. This chakra is directly linked to the highest energetic vibration, which is love.

Your heart is your transformation center. The energetic components of your thoughts are transferred to the Heart Chakra, which are experienced as feelings. Emotions are feelings (senses) that become charged with passion and intention, and this combination of thoughts and emotions are the driving force behind creative manifestation.

Chakra #5 – The Vishuddhi, Throat Chakra

Your voice is a powerful and versatile medium for your expression of free will, which translates your thoughts, emotions, and ideas into action. Your Throat Chakra delivers intentions through the invocation of sound, which is expressed in various ways such as by speaking, yelling, screaming, singing, chanting, humming, or playing musical instruments.

We block the natural energetic flow to this portal when we avoid standing up for ourselves, or when we refuse to tell others how we feel. If we allow fear to dominate over self-expression because we worry what someone might think, this can lead to the experience of having a "lump in the throat".

The "lump in the throat" sensation signals that we are blocking the life force energy from flowing through this chakra. We do not need to be reactionary, loud, or forceful to get our message across. All we need to do is stay true to ourselves by not being afraid to proclaim who we are and what we stand for. This is all that is required to be in alignment with the energetic flow to this chakra.

Worrying about what other people think when you share your beliefs, values, and feelings is a road to nowhere, because you do not have the power to make another person happy. It is always another person's choice whether they want to experience happiness or not.

The energetic vibration of happiness and inner joy is contagious though, because it is genuine. When you feel blissful and true to yourself, this will encourage others to do the same. The greatest love you can give to someone else is to love yourself by being yourself.

Don't put on a fake mask and claim that to be your true self, because you think that people will like this version of you more than the real you. When you do this, you are living selfishly, because you are not sharing the person you were meant to be with others. When you stand up for what you believe, speak clearly of your boundaries, expose your vulnerabilities, and share your insights, you are giving the greatest version of yourself to others.

No one benefits when you live in ways that are obligatory, self-sacrificing, or when you bend your truth in order to please another person. Remember, the way to love others unconditionally is to unconditionally love yourself, which is by expressing yourself as fully as you can, just the way you are. One of the greatest modes of self-expression is honoring yourself through the power of your voice.

Chakra #6 – The Third Eye, Brow Chakra

This chakra is located between your eyes and browline, and is linked to the pineal gland, or the third eye. The third eye or the three "i's" associated with this chakra are *imagination, intuition,* and *insight,* because your third eye has the ability to perceive or "see" beyond ordinary physical sight. Psychics, mediums, clairvoyants, visionaries, artists, remote viewers, or those who have lucid dreams are comfortable using their third eye to see. Interestingly, this sixth chakra is also commonly referred to as the sixth sense.

The pineal gland is a tiny gland responsible for sleep and wake cycles by producing melatonin, which is the hormone necessary for inducing sleep and regulating states of consciousness, such as the induction of dreams or meditative states – all which open the doorway to metaphysical experiences. Ancient Egyptians, Druidics, Hindus, Hasidics, Islamics, Taoists, Mayans, Tibetans and the Aboriginal cultures all understood the pineal gland to be a powerful, all-seeing third eye that is linked to a higher, spiritual dimension.[21] It was later discovered by scientists that the pineal gland has retinal tissue composed of rods and cones, or photoreceptors, similar to an actual eye.[22]

The United States government has even taken an interest in third eye "seeing". There is an all-seeing eye printed on the American dollar bill, and millions of dollars have been spent on remote viewing programs such as SCANATE and Project Star Gate, which were used in military operations for more than 20 years, beginning in 1972.[23] Law enforcement has relied on psychics and remote viewers in their investigations for decades as a method for investigating crime, finding perpetrators, or locating victims.

Ancient civilizations and those in positions of power have sought ways to activate the sixth chakra called the third eye, while at the same time, mainstream society has been misguided or led to believe that there is no such thing as a third eye or even a sixth sense. Because of the third eye's relationship to the pineal gland, and the power this bestows in our ability to see into the future, and connect to higher spiritual realms, there has been a deliberate attempt to calcify or reduce the effectiveness of one's pineal gland by adding fluoride to civilian food and water.

Since the pineal gland stores more fluoride in the body than any of the other organs, bones, or teeth, the key to allowing energy to move through this chakra is to eliminate fluoride exposure. There are fluoride free toothpastes that you can purchase, and drinking fluoridated water should also be avoided.

Eating an organic diet, while avoiding processed foods that contain refined sugars or white flour, and avoiding soda will prevent tooth decay, naturally. Drinking green and black teas and eating apples have also been proven to remove plaque build-up. We cannot depend on mainstream medicine or The American Dental Association to inspire healthier eating as a means of promoting the overall health of the body, bones, and teeth, because while we know this is true, there has also been a hyper-focus on perpetuating the idea that ingesting toxins, poisons, and unnatural chemicals is somehow beneficial. We have to make choices that are coherent with what our common sense tells us, because when looking to the large establishments for guidance, common sense always takes a back seat to profit and other hidden agendas.

Chakra #7 – The Crown Chakra

The Crown Chakra is the seventh chakra located at the top of the head. This is where the life force energy enters the body and is dispersed to all the lower chakras. Some people can feel this powerful, life force energy as an intelligence that moves through them, which is described as having the physical sensation of tingles or goose bumps, which starts at the top of the head and moves down the back of the neck, spine, and finally to the extremities.

Those that have experienced this sensation of energy moving through their crown chakra mention that it can happen while listening to music that is emotionally moving and inspiring, or it can happen when you receive information from another person or from your higher self, whereby you feel that your soul has been given a deeper level of information. It feels as though your entire being lights up with love and wisdom, and there are no words to describe it.

The universe is a creative, intelligent universe that originated from thought. All thought, just like sound, light, and everything else that ever materialized, was created from a larger creative mind. You did not create thought. You get to experience thought and the act of thinking. You get to choose the thoughts you will have, but you are not the original creator of thought. Therefore, thoughts do not originate within your own mind in a vacuum. Your brain acts as a receiver, your heart serves as your guide, and your consciousness chooses the types of thoughts you will experience. Thoughts are energy and the thoughts you have do not begin and end with you.

For example, have you ever had an intrusive thought enter your mind that simply wasn't appealing and you asked yourself, "Where did that thought come from? I didn't want to experience that!" Have you ever been with a person who was in a bad mood and their negative attitude and stress rubbed off on you? Likewise, have you ever been to a class or seminar and the positive energy you received from the presenter led you towards a path of having new insights and thoughts that you didn't have before?

We don't realize that we are constantly choosing to accept or let go of thoughts that 'enter' our mind all the time. The very statement of "having a thought 'enter' our mind" reminds us that thoughts are capable of entering the mind, literally, and this happens to all of us whether we are conscious of it or not.

There is an invisible field where thoughts can be manifested and transferred from. This field is where creative ideas spring, where insights and inspirations come from, and where intuitive connections with others reside. We are all connected to this external energetic field of thought and your physical brain is simply a receiver and a processor.

This does not mean that you don't have free will. Your free will is always there, and is part of your consciousness. You are constantly deciding and sorting what thoughts you will choose to have and when. Moreover, when you have a thought, the pathways in your brain become re-wired to make new connections, which continue to absorb similar patterns of thought. Positive thoughts will attract more positive thoughts and negative thoughts will do the same.

When you are in a good mood, you are choosing to entertain positive thoughts. In doing so, you will proceed to move forward in an upward direction by having increasingly more positive thoughts, which will lead you to experience feelings of joy, contentment, and enthusiasm. Likewise, by choosing to focus on negative thoughts, your mind can spiral into a state of depression, and you will experience increasingly more negative thoughts and situations, because the patterns in your brain will wire itself to support whatever you focus on.

There are only two modes of thought: Positive or negative. There are different forms and degrees of the two, but any thoughts you have always stem from one of the two opposing vibrations. Which type of thought do you wish to invite into your space?

Higher vibrational thoughts are positive and will always connect you to the higher mind, because the cosmic mind is positive by nature. When you are open to positive thoughts, you will find creativity and oneness in the thoughts that flow to you. This higher form of thinking is channeled through your crown chakra, connecting you to infinite possibilities. Higher thinking is non-judgmental, unconditionally loving, and operates out of faith and trust. When you choose to side with and harbor thoughts that are positive, you will be in sync with the greater cosmic mind, and you can gage this because emotionally, you will feel good, healthy, and energized.

When you feel tired, depressed, angry, or boxed into a corner, it is because the thoughts you are inviting into your mind are negative. We can use our moods and feelings as a barometer to gage the thoughts we are having, whether they are positive or negative. We are not always conscious of our thoughts, because some dwell in our subconscious mind, but we are conscious of our moods and feelings. Any corresponding feelings will always follow thoughts, so paying attention to your feelings will help you recognize the types of thoughts you are having. If you want to change your mood, simply change your thoughts.

Lower vibrational thinking comes from our own negative ego that forms and responds to our own false beliefs and irrational fears. Negative thinking blocks the positive vibrational energy from coming into the crown chakra, because negative thinking is restrictive, critical and limiting. Blocking your life force energy with toxic thoughts is the same as choosing to put junk food in your body that is laced with chemicals.

Disease, means without ease. Just as we can starve ourselves nutritionally by eating an unhealthy diet, we can also starve ourselves from our connection to the life force energy by choosing negative thoughts instead of positive thoughts. Remember that we cannot hold two opposing thoughts in our mind at the same time. If we choose to focus on fear and lack, we cannot also harbor thoughts of love and safety in that same moment.

In every moment, you are making a decision within the polarity of thought. The more positive thoughts you choose and the more positive people you surround yourself with, the more you will be aligned with the universal mind, and this will connect you to the true nature of who you are. Staying in a positive frame of mind will allow the life force energy to move and work through you, and this will not only help you ascend and grow, but the light you radiate, will influence and affect all those you come into contact with.

Energy is always in motion, transforming and expanding. Since thoughts and emotions are forms of energy that move through you, it is important to know that your thoughts and emotions can influence others around you. Everything is connected by a vibratory network of energy that is held together by a common thread. There is one collective energetic field of energy that connects and unifies all frequencies to one source. You contribute to this energetic field, either positively or negatively, depending on the types of thoughts and emotions that vibrate from your being. The more you express love to others no matter what situation you encounter, the more you will match the frequency of love within the collective field. Energetically, this means you will see more love, feel more love, experience more love, because you will match this frequency within the collective field of consciousness.

There is one letter in the word "your" that when removed, becomes "our". It is the letter "y" which is the "why" that keeps creeping into our mind, clouding our sense of connection to All That Is. When we allow our mind to be flooded with questions that express self-loathing such as *"why me?"* or *"why is this happening?"*, we become critical and our thinking becomes driven by our ego, instead of our higher mind.

It is good to be inquisitive and ask questions, but when we ask questions so that we can label everything as YOURS or MINE, JUST or UNJUST, GOOD or BAD, then this takes us away from our connection to the common thread. In reality, it is OUR planet, OUR stars, OUR breath, OUR thoughts, and OUR life. When we know this, we will experience peace and harmony. The connection to All That Is, is who we really are, and this is where we will find a greater sense of joy and peace.

CHAPTER TWO

YOU ARE WHOLE. YOU ARE ONE

Dear One,

You have been led to believe that you are less than the one who created you, when in fact; you are a mirrored replica of your creator. There is one consciousness or one intelligence that exists at the core of all living things. We will call this 'The I AM Presence'.

The I AM presence is your connection to All That Is. All That Is comes from and originates from energy, from one source, and from one mind. It is the whole and it is also the parts. This concept can be compared to knowing that every cell in your body has the DNA that holds the blueprint reflective of your entire body. You hold the blueprint within yourself that also reflects the same blueprint that is within the body of creation.

All That Is has a vibration and a voice of its own just like you, and it also can be heard as the voice of many. The individual parts of the whole have their own jobs and their own place and it must exist this way, otherwise All That Is cannot be all that it expresses itself to be.

You are an individual fractal that has branched off directly from the whole. Fractals hold the exact mathematical proportions as the whole, which is why it is important that you be yourself as fully as you can so you can express yourself exactly as you were created to be. This is the only way that All That Is can come to know its infinite nature and unveil its own expression.

The cells in your body serve a specific purpose and the individual cells or "parts" benefit the "whole", or the entire body, when all the cells are doing what they have been designed to do. Do you know what happens to the body if any of the individual cells refuse to follow their DNA blueprint?

You are one cell in the body of creation. It is important to BE exactly who you are, to follow your bliss and your calling exactly as this defines you in your own unique way so that you can fearlessly BE the individual you were designed to be. Do not compare yourself to anyone else. When you live as the person you were meant to be, you will be expressing your highest and greatest good and this also serves the good, health, and well-being of the whole.

You are the greatest gift that the world could ever see and know, when you are you, just as you are. Do not try to be anyone else. Do not try to think like anyone else. Do not try to behave like someone else. There is an entire world of other bodies or other cells that are dependent on you to do your job and this will trigger them to do their job as part of the total body of creation. Your only job is to be you. Therein lies the beautiful and wondrous creation of you — you as an individual, you as a fractal of the whole, and you as the whole itself. This is the nature of who you truly are.

Transcribed From:
The Voice of Creation

. . . .

"There are three classes of people: Those who see, those who see when they are shown, and those who do not see." – *Leonardo da Vinci*

Once upon a time, there was a solid sphere of light and this light was named Consciousness. Although Consciousness was self-aware, intelligent, and understood that it was synonymous with the vibration of love, it did not fully know what it was capable of and to what extent it could experience its own love, because the only love it knew was contained within itself. Consciousness decided to divide so it could replicate itself into countless parts. This became the offspring of Consciousness and Consciousness named its offspring, Free Will.

Free Will Beings could experience anything they wanted and desired. They could experience being as far away from Consciousness's original vibration of love as they desired and some of them even killed and destroyed one another in order to achieve the experience of feeling separate and alone. Other Free Will Beings replicated the vibration of love in everything they co-created, and they saw this was beautiful. Some Free Will Beings wanted to experience a rainbow of colorful feelings and drama so they could express their aliveness as fully as they could. There was nothing that the Free Will Beings could not become, achieve, or experience.

After awhile, the Free Will Beings realized that their freedom to choose how they were expressing themselves did not accurately define who they were. Their individual experiences were not defining them. Their choices were not defining them. Their desires were not defining them. No matter how individualized they became, they kept asking the same questions to one another, "Who am I? Where did I come from? What am I doing here?" It did not matter what they accomplished, what they believed in, what they sought after, or what they experienced. These questions remained unanswered until one day...

One of the Free Will Beings announced, "I know who I am! I know where I came from, and I know what I am doing here!"

All of the other Free Will Beings paused whatever they were doing and listened, and this Free Will Being continued to share his insight. "I am who you are. I came from where you came from, and I am here because you are here. I know this because I can see that no matter how different we are, we always have one thing in common."

This Free Will Being pointed to the center of his chest and within the very next heartbeat, a light began to beam out from his heart. This beam of light touched the heart of all the other Free Will Beings, and then they began to notice that they also had this light within themselves.

Rays of light beamed brightly from the core of every Free Will Being that it did not matter how dark things were for those who drifted farthest away from Consciousness. It did not matter what unique experiences each Free Will Being had. It did not matter what someone did or did not do. The light continued to radiate out from every being, because the awareness of this light is what illuminated it.

As soon as the Free Will Beings saw this light within themselves, it lit the path so they could find their way home. As each Free Will Being started to return home, they began to share all of their stories and unique experiences with Consciousness and with one another.

When Consciousness listened to all of their stories, and heard all the ways they could express their individualization, Consciousness smiled and said, "Thank you for showing me all the ways I could express myself. I could not have done this without you."

All the Free Will Beings were swooped back into the arms of Consciousness and a new type of consciousness was born called, *"All That Is"*. This became a unified experience that everyone could rejoice in. Separation became unity and unity became separation, all within the same breath of Consciousness.

The above story illustrates how everything is one and one is everything. Separation and duality are illusions, because nothing (no thing) can ever really be separate from the whole.

The reason we experience the illusion of separation and duality is because, All That Is cannot be all that it is without having the free will to express everything it can be. However, once we see all the ways we are unified in sameness with one another, instead of focusing on how we are different, we will notice wholeness within ourselves.

Individualization has always been part of wholeness and not separate from it. When you see that you are a unique expression of creation, characterized by your free will, emanating as a beam of light that vibrates within you and through you, you will begin to see this same light illuminated in everyone else. You will know that one is all and all is one.

My Experience Of Coming Home

While on my journey of writing this book, I was woken from sleep one night and became aware that someone was speaking to me telepathically. I recognized it as, The Voice of Creation. It was the same voice I heard when I began writing the beginning of each chapter. It was the same voice that asked me to write down "The Seven Principles of I AM".

This time, this voice asked me a question: "Would you like to experience All That Is?"

I immediately felt afraid. From my ego's perspective, I thought I would lose my sense of self if I experienced *All That Is*, or even worse, I would cease to exist completely. I thanked the voice for the offer, as I fearfully answered, "No. I don't want to experience that, because if I did, I would lose my identity."

The voice continued, "You won't lose your identity. You will still exist. When you experience All That Is, you will be in your natural, original state of existence. If you want to experience All That Is right now, all you have to do is let go of your fear and acknowledge that you are ONE with All That Is."

I paused in apprehension. I still felt afraid but I also knew I was safe in the presence of this voice, so I decided to surrender my fear and explore what The Voice of Creation came to show me. I took a breath and replied steadfastly, "I acknowledge that I am one with All

That Is."

In that moment, I experienced a shifting in all the boundaries that separated me from everything else in the universe. My conscious awareness was released from the constructs of linear space and time; and within seconds, I saw and felt everything in creation whirling before me at lightening fast speed.

I felt like I was in some type of spiraling vortex, because I had the sensation of spinning but not in the sense that I felt any vertigo. The spinning sensation was very fast, lasting for just a few seconds, and then suddenly, I experienced a kind of stillness and silence that was as though time stood still.

In the midst of silent, timeless, suspension, I experienced my consciousness in everything. I was detached by a field of empty space, while I simultaneously became conscious of my existence as every living cell, every atom, every grain of sand, every human soul, every animal, the water, the plants, the earth, the stars, and every single element ever created, all at once.

The experience was brief, but powerful. It seems as though it should have taken much longer to experience this degree of expansion in consciousness. I went from having one central point of consciousness as defined by the self, to having a multidimensional, unlimited meld with consciousness that spread into every living thing that has ever been created.

It is unfathomable to comprehend how this could be possible from our limited logical understanding, and to communicate this experience in written words cannot fully illustrate what it was like. Nonetheless, experiencing a unified consciousness, even just momentarily, was life altering. After that experience, I started to see an aspect of myself in every living thing. I no longer needed to be convinced that the idea of separation was just a grand illusion. I now had the personal experience to know that unity consciousness is real, and it can be obtained and experienced even while living in this human form.

One Consciousness Divided

At the heart of consciousness, we exist as ONE. We exist in everything, but because we have chosen physical existence, one consciousness has spread out and divided into parts so we could have the free will to choose our own form of expression, experience co-creation, and become the individualized versions of consciousness that we are.

In order for us to exist as physical beings in physical reality, we had to "label" our understanding of the world and we adapted a belief system where *we think* there is separatism and duality. We understand there is light and dark; good and bad; male and female. However, we tend to place our focus on what is separate instead of what is whole, although both exist at the same time.

The more we focus on how we are unified and connected to one another, the more we will remember our true nature, before we became fractals of the whole. It is simply a matter of choosing what part of our consciousness we wish to experience – our self as the one, or our self as separate from one another. Our point of consciousness and what we choose to acknowledge and believe is what will create the reality we experience.

The Divine Masculine And Feminine

In recent history, we have acknowledged *the differences* between men and women more often than we have embraced the masculine and feminine qualities within ourselves. When examining the divine feminine, as opposed to the socially constructed concept of what is feminine, we know that the divine feminine is characterized by traits exhibited by the right side of the brain. This is the intuitive part of us.

Feminine energy is compassionate, loving and nurturing. It is receptive, creative, and life bearing.

The divine masculine is characterized by traits in the left side of the brain. It is the logical thinker. Masculine energy is instrumental in solving problems. It is protective, life giving, and productive.

The masculine and the feminine are two energies that actually operate as one. When all traits are recognized as being equally important, the two energies will work in harmony.

The majority of recent civilizations have rejected the divine feminine and the divine masculine and replaced it with a false construct of what is male and what is female. Gender roles have portrayed that anything feminine is negative or unimportant, while anything considered masculine is more desirable. As a result, women have suffered with more poverty and experienced more discrimination and abuse than their male counterparts.

Both men and women have been discouraged from behaving in ways that exercise too much feminine energy. For example, it's not considered socially appropriate to be too nurturing, too intuitive, or too spiritual, but one can never be too logical or too scientific. When making decisions in the workplace or when being taught to solve problems academically, scientific reasoning is encouraged over intuition.

Studies in math, the hard sciences, and medicine are valued and result in better paying jobs compared to studies in the creative arts. Most teachers, caregivers, and artists are paid poorly, while chemists, lawyers, and surgeons are paid well.

Both sexes are encouraged to focus on producing more, working harder, and to use only the left side of the brain to logically solve problems as opposed to exercising any creativity, emotions, or intuition. The social imbalance has pulled us away from knowing how we can work with these two powerful energies within ourselves.

Society has created a false sense of what is masculine and what is feminine and this has fueled the illusion of separatism instead of bringing us closer to our unity. When we combine the creative, intuitive mind with the productive, logical mind, the two halves of the brain join together to become one.

The right hemisphere of the brain exhibits traits that are considered feminine and operates creatively, focusing on the wholeness instead of the parts, while the left hemisphere exhibits traits that are considered to be masculine, operating logically, analytically, sequentially, and focuses on the parts of the whole. The two halves of the brain are equally important. One is not better than the other.

You are whole because you are the "yin" and the "yang", which means that two opposing forces are actually complimentary and necessary in order to bring forth completeness and wholeness. There is an inter-dynamic relationship throughout the universe, in which the whole is the actual system. The perception that there are separate parts, working against the other, deludes us away from the truth. Everything is whole. Everything is one.

Fractals And The Micro/Macro Connection

Inside your body, there lives a universe made of tiny cells to form organs, and each organ provides its own specific function, working in harmony with every other organ. Each one of your cells contains the entire blueprint to create your whole body. The micro is the macro.

Your heart beats 100,000 times a day or about 35 million times a year.[24] Your lungs take in oxygen at every breath and this oxygen is transported throughout the bloodstream so it can be delivered to every cell in your body. Your stomach, liver, gallbladder, pancreas and intestines all work together to extract nutrients from the food you eat. Your body heals and repairs itself everyday. You do not need to be consciously aware of any of these functions in order for this system to operate efficiently. This is a perfect expression of independent parts working together to create a whole system. Nothing happens in isolation. All the parts work together to complete a larger system, which is a powerhouse of energy: Your healthy body. We find this same biological model in all of creation, where the sum of the parts and the replication of systems are necessary in order to create an entire, larger system.

This miraculous design of the body, in which smaller parts make up the whole, is repeated in every living person all over the world, and in other species throughout nature. Everything in nature and in creation is made up of sequences and patterns, which are derived from basic mathematical principles.

(Figure – 5)

Image of a Mandelbrot Set

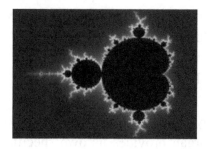

Benoit Mandelbrot coined the term "fractals" and used "fractal geometry" to describe a visual design that occurs with the repetition of patterns. To create this design, a shape must be divided into parts to form smaller copies of itself, so that every aspect of the design is similar in magnification.[25]

Clouds, coastlines, plants, seashells, the strands of our DNA, and every unique snowflake that ever took form are fractals. The smaller portion of a snowflake is an exact replica of the entire snowflake, and these geometric patterns are expressed in everything, from the smallest particle to the entire universe.

This image, viewed from space, shows the natural fractal patterns on earth.

Curated from Google Earth by professor Paul Bourke. [26]

(Figure – 6)

Fractal patterns are found consistently in nature:
(Figures 7 -9) [27]

 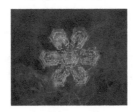 

(Figure 7)   (Figure 8)   (Figure 9)

Scientists have discovered that the mathematical sequences represented in nature are the same mathematical sequences found in the Fibonacci calculations, which were discovered around 1200AD, by an Italian mathematician, Leonardo Pisano. This Fibonacci number sequence includes the consecutive addition of the first two numbers in which the sum of the first two, generates the third number. The Fibonacci sequence is formulated as follows: 0+1=1; 1+1=2; 1+2=3; 2+3=5; 3+5=8; 5+8=13; 8+13=21; 13+21=34; 21+34=55; and so on, in which the sum creates a sequence of this partial list of numbers (1, 2, 3, 5, 8, 13, 21, 34, 55, 89, 144...), which could go on to infinity. These same repeated patterns exist in nature, creating an array of fractal geometric patterns.[28]

A numeric value known as "Phi", was named after Phidias, a Greek sculptor. Ancient Greek architects used a mathematical ratio of proportions now known as "Phi", to build their buildings and monuments, which is a ratio or proportion of 1.618... This number happens to be based on the same methods used to formulate the Fibonacci sequence. The aesthetically pleasing quality of architecture created by the Greeks was based on this formula, which gave rise to the names used to describe this as the Golden Section, the Golden Ratio, or the Golden Mean.[29]

Leonardo da Vinci also understood the Golden Ratio and created his paintings by relying on what he referred to as "divine proportion". The measurements found in da Vinci paintings consistently followed ratios based on this Golden Ratio.[29]

The proportions of your own body are based on Phi plus the number 5. For example, you have five fingers and five toes on each side of your body, and each one of your fingers consists of three joints. The combined value of the distance between the first smaller joint and the middle joint equals the sum of the largest finger joint. The length of your hand has the combined value of Phi when measured with the forearm. The proportions that make up every dimension of your face are also equal to Phi. For example, the spatial distance between your eyes, from your eye to the tip of your ear, and even the proportions of your teeth are all permutations of Phi.[30]

These same sets of ratios based on this rule of proportion occur throughout nature, in music, in the visual arts, in architecture... in everything! Some have said that God is a mathematician and uses a coded language found consistently in every aspect of creation. There is plenty of evidence to show that there is a mathematical blueprint found throughout the expression of life. There is no randomness when we observe the creation of nature, because everything that exists in our universe was based on a set of sequences that replicated the sequences before it. The very design of life is not only replicating, but has been precisely replicated in the form of geometric patterns that follow mathematical principles.

Our human brain is also wired by this same sequence, which explains why we find beauty when we look at nature. We recognize sequences and patterns, even when things appear to be random, although we are not consciously aware of this. When we look at a flower, a coastline, or a mountain range, we all agree that nature is incredibly beautiful.

A fractal relationship has also been discovered at the quantum, subatomic level. Quantum Entanglement is a scientific discovery that demonstrates how two separate subatomic particles affect one another no matter how far apart the two particles are. In other words, when an observer, measures the spin of particle A, particle B will also give the same measurement once it is observed, regardless of how far apart the two entangled particles are. Something invisible seems to link them as if they are one and the same.[31]

The universal blueprint of creation is that it is holographic, because fractalization exists at every level, both energetically and physically. A hologram is whole and complete onto itself, while at the same time; it is part of a greater pattern. The micro reflects and affects the macro and the macro reflects and affects the micro. A single change in one aspect, affects the entire pattern. This creative mechanism continues to spiral down to the smallest degree, while it holds the same form, shape, and function of its larger counterparts.

Understanding The Macro And Micro Relationship In Creation and Evolution

Creation and evolution are synonymous. Creation is constantly evolving and evolution is always creating and expanding. You cannot have one without the other, and yet, Evolutionists and Creationists continue to battle over this as if it can only be one way or the other, when in fact, the two paradigms are synonymous.

The development of the human embryo occurs in stages that mimic evolution. There is a Big Bang when the sperm meets the egg and the beginning of life starts as a single-celled organism. The cells become specialized as they divide and the embryo develops the appearance of gill slits, which resembles aquatic life. Then, the embryo takes on a reptilian-like appearance and forms a tail. As the embryo develops into a fetus, it begins to look more mammal-like, until it is finally recognizable as a human being. From an evolutionary perspective, we see the macro expressed within the micro, as the same stages of evolution on our planet are duplicated during human gestation.

The recipe for life, prior to its manifestation, has already been thought of and designed as if it were a drawing or a blueprint. DNA contains the entire blueprint for that which will be physically expressed at the time of conception. The literal meaning of the word, "conceive" means "to think or create something in the mind." Whose mind or what mind thought our existence into reality when we were conceived? The blueprint that exists in DNA tells us there was a design for our existence.

Micro and macro relationships not only occur in nature, but they are also replicated energetically in everything we do as a collective species based on the individual actions we take. For example, when we gather information to learn new things as individuals, we are also influencing the intellectual evolution within the human species on a macro scale. Whether we make a scientific discovery, create a recipe, come up with a new invention, or make technological advancements, we are affecting humanity's intellectual evolution.

Our collective advancement occurs in stages, because in order to expand on new ideas, inventions, and insights, we must borrow information from another person's previous ideas or discoveries so that we can expand on the information that already exists. Nothing is created in a vacuum or in isolation.

As a species, we are expanding and growing collectively, just as we are doing individually. We have seen technology take a massive leap during the 21st century, because more people are tapping into and contributing to already existing knowledge. The wide-use of the Internet has accelerated the individual's ability to influence and contribute to the larger pool of information, leading to further advancements at even faster rates.

When we think we are working alone or acting independently, we are actually either affected by or impacting the larger collective. For example, when you talk to another person, share an idea, or give a gift, you cannot know how your actions impact the other person, nor will you know about the countless other people that your acts of kindness may have influenced as well.

There is a rippling effect that occurs whenever you have an interaction with just one person, because there is always a chain reaction that follows every action. Once you understand how one person affects many, you can understand that you, as one individual, have the potential to affect hundreds, thousands, or even millions of people. When you change just one thing about yourself, you ARE changing the world. Your choices, decisions, and any actions you take will lead to your own evolution, and this in turn, affects the evolution for all of humanity.

Being conscious of what you think, what you choose to do, and how you live your life is extremely important, because your actions affect humanity as a whole. You are part of the collective consciousness. You are part of the whole, because you are the whole. Your very existence and state of being is always connected to All That Is. We are constantly evolving, growing and learning on every level – physically, mentally, and spiritually, both as individuals and as a collective. This is the blueprint for life, because creation and evolution are synonymous.

Oneness In The Eyes Of A Child

You may not remember when you were a small child, but if you are a parent, grandparent, or caregiver of children, you will be reminded of unity consciousness whenever you observe the way children play and interact with one another. Children are still connected to their natural state of oneness, because they have had less exposure to social influences, thereby not giving the ego enough time to fully crystalize a false sense of self.

My son, Cameron, has reminded my husband and I of our connection to All That Is on many occasions. One such occasion occurred one beautiful August afternoon, a few weeks before the start of Cameron's fourth grade school year when we decided to take a drive to the Oregon coast. My husband and I anticipated a long walk along the beach to get some exercise, but Cameron had better things in mind.

With the splashing of waves, sand castles that needed to be built and seashells that needed to be discovered, our son was completely distracted and not the least bit interested in the idea of getting some exercise. He knew that he could play and exercise at the same time. If all he did was just walk along the beach, he would miss the chance to completely submerge himself in the beauty that surrounded him.

Cameron didn't want to walk along the beach and let the waves occasionally wash over his feet. He wanted to experience the full power of the ocean by running and splashing against the rising and receding tides as they crashed around his body. He rolled in the sand and picked up every seashell he found, as if it was calling out to him by name. He played in a timeless state of consciousness, and the only thing that could pull him away from his feeling of oneness would be when his parents announced that it was time to go. While my husband and I watched our son play on the beach, our own hearts filled with joy and contentment, because he was helping us remember our oneness with All That Is, even if we weren't consciously aware of this.

We noticed a mother and her two young boys spread out a blanket and some sand toys near where Cameron was playing. Cameron immediately took notice of the two other boys and started playing with them. They bonded instantly and within less than five minutes, the three new playmates were walking together arm in arm. They acted as though they had known each other for years, having no regard for physical boundaries, judgments or worries, and the children had only met minutes ago.

I realized how interesting it was that my husband and I had not even introduced ourselves to the mother of the boys who sat near us, and it would be completely socially inappropriate for me to put my arm around the other mother this soon after meeting her, even if we had introduced ourselves. When children are in an environment that allows them to express themselves in the most carefree ways, they live in oneness with nature, with themselves, and with one another. This is our true nature and the nature we were born with.

When Oneness Eludes Us

What happens to that feeling of connection once when we reach adulthood? Why does it become so difficult when we grow older to lose ourselves in timeless play and remain in the present moment for any length of time? What causes us to feel separate instead of unified with one another, when oneness is our natural state of being that we are born with knowing?

There has been an agenda behind the scenes to purposefully block you from maintaining your awareness of your true self – with the intention that you will forget your connection to oneness and to All That Is. The reason is because when you forget your connection to oneness and believe that you are separate, you become easier to control.

It is easier to control individuals who live in fear, believe they are victims of circumstance, and who feel separate and divided from one another, because when people feel powerless in their own lives, they are literally inviting others to hold power over them. We live in a free will universe that will reflect back what we believe to be true. Physical reality is like a mirror. If you believe that you can't do something, that you are less than someone else, disadvantaged, weak, frail, or vulnerable, then you are asking for the universe to reflect this reality back to you. The universe will materialize whatever you hold true within your core beliefs, because it is through consciousness and perception that physical reality is experienced. The idea that "seeing is believing" should be rephrased as "believing is seeing", because the later is more accurate.

Therefore, whenever you hold onto the belief that you are separate, alone, fragmented, incomplete, or not good enough, you are adapting to a belief system that is characteristic of one who lacks power in their life. There will always be someone who will prove that your perception is correct. Alternately, when you remember your oneness and how your are equal to everyone and everything, because you hold the same light that is in All That Is, there can never be any person or circumstance that can have power over you.

What if everyone paid attention to "The Link" and noticed that a vibration of love threads us to each other and this thread is always there? What if everyone lived fearlessly because we trusted one another, and we were all aware of our connection, not only to each other, but to the entire universe? We would live once again like children. There would be no need for a money system, because there would not be any competition for resources. There would be no reason to have war and conflict, because we would have explicit trust and connection to everyone and everything.

By maintaining this awareness and by simply choosing kindness and acceptance over dissension, by choosing peace and love instead of conflict and resentment, and by choosing to let go of fear because each of us knows that nothing can exist outside the body of creation, then we will have taken our power back. However, since this ideology is still perceived to be unprocurable for most people, then it is easy to understand why the masses keep fostering ideas of separatism, lack, and discontentment. This has been the more real ideology, so that is what we continue to experience as a collective.

Separation is just an illusion and out of this illusion, an artificially constructed sense of self has been molded into existence known as the ego. The ego's sense of self has been further reinforced and magnified in the way that society has been structured. For example, in order to create consumers, marketers devise commercials on television, and elsewhere, to encourage feelings of dissatisfaction. The ego is repeatedly fed the idea that one cannot be good enough, wealthy enough, happy enough, attractive enough, or smart enough without the latest gadget or product. If one does not have enough money to buy the latest gadget or product, then more feelings of unworthiness follow, attaching the belief that your job or level of income defines your worth as a human being. Then, more commercials are aired, encouraging the use of antidepressants to fix the problem of depression, which the ego-feeding commercials contributed to in the first place.

Turning off the TV is not a bad idea. I stopped watching TV years ago to minimize my exposure to all the rhetoric, and miraculously, my feelings of self-worth improved. I can easily find news on the Internet instead. From there, I can choose what I want to read and separate the truth from the hype. Ever since I turned off the TV, I found that I haven't missed anything.

The global banking cartel and the top one percent (elitists), who own most of the stock and operate the largest corporations, want to remain in power. However, in order to remain in power, there has to be an agreeable populace. There cannot be power over anyone unless an individual believes they are powerless or less powerful than they actually are. The idea of powerlessness is taught. This is not the human condition that you were born with.

How Separatism, Lack, And Powerlessness Is Taught

We were not born feeling separate from anyone or anything. As children, we knew our connection to All That Is. When looking at nature, there is always connection, interdependence, and balance. We know that nature does not operate out of separatism and we are all part of nature. The idea that we are separate and unequal to one another is an artificially constructed ideology, which is part of the agenda to control the population, but we do not have to buy into this.

We all have the free will to choose our own thoughts and beliefs. That is why this type of insidious control is possible, because the agenda feeds out of the belief that our free will has not been violated; so it does not seem natural to think of ourselves as being enslaved. You may own your own home, have the freedom to decide what you want to eat or drink each day, decide where you want to live, select the career of your choice, decide who you will marry, and so on. It may seem like you have all the freedom in the world and you can do whatever you want; however, when you look deeper, you will begin to notice that your freedom has been violated, because you and everyone else has been told what the human condition is, and it's not the one you were born with. We do not realize this is happening on any conscious level, because we have all been willing participants.

If we believe we are powerless in our abilities to manifest what we want, and if we remain detached from the infinite nature of our unified consciousness, then we are easier to enslave. This manipulation has been going on for thousands of years and it is perpetuated through the following means: We are manipulated mentally, spiritually, and emotionally, and made to feel that we are far less powerful than we are.

Mental Disempowerment

Mental disempowerment begins within our educational system, where critical thinking and creativity have been discouraged. Subjects in the creative arts, music, sports, and physical education have been removed from the curriculum in most American schools. These are subjects that strengthen one's spirit – allowing for creative expression. Recreation encourages social bonding and reinforces unity and oneness. Instead of fostering creative, independent thinkers or building community relationships, a child's education has been whittled down to nothing other more than rigorous testing, and the regurgitation of facts through rote memorization.

The grading system that schools use to measure progress is based on rewarding and punishing children by conditioning them that memorization and following rules is positive and that anything else will result in poor test scores or failing grades. The obsession over test scores and achieving high grades as opposed to striving for a love of learning disrupts our natural connection to "The Link" that we are all born with. The more the ego is fed the idea that it is separate and powerless during these early years, the easier it is to forget who we truly are. We have been taught to do what others want us to do instead of following our heart. We forget that we live in a universe that is actually listening to us, that always brings forth what we think and believe about ourselves into physical manifestation. When we are taught that we are separate, we fall asleep and forget who we are; and without any awareness, we willingly give our power away by believing the messages we are told over and over again: The false message is that we are powerless.

The No Child Left Behind Act passed by the Bush Administration in 2001, led to many of the budget cuts in the creative arts, music, sports and physical education. On the surface, this law sounds very nice and like our government cares about children, which is characteristic of most laws in order to get the masses to agree and go along with an agenda. What this law is really saying to our schools is, "Do what we tell you, or you won't receive any money from us."

Even if teachers wanted to teach subjects that they know would enhance their students' learning, the system has been designed so that there is no time for anything other than rigorous academics. The student's ability to score well in reading and math tests determines whether or not a school will qualify for federal funding. This leaves the school districts with no other choice but to push teachers and students to score as high as they can on achievement tests. The best way to accomplish this is to remove any other subjects that might interfere, which is why we have seen the gradual removal of studies in the creative arts, music, and physical education.

The law states that in order for any school in America to receive federal funding, schools must give assessments to all students of all grade levels, which includes annual testing, academic progress reports, report cards, and teacher qualifications.[32] "States have restructured curriculum, increased training requirements for teachers and implemented standardized tests, all to boost reading and math performance as required by the law. Critics claim that the focus on reading and math has taken time away from other important subjects and that current tests are a high-pressure but incomplete measure of student achievement."[33] According to a 2012 Gallup poll, only 28 percent of Americans believe that "The No Child Left Behind Act" has improved the educational system, while 48 percent of Americans believe this law has resulted in the decline of public education.[34]

Attempts to keep us feeling separate, unworthy, and powerless to change our situation, continue after high school and into college. With the rising costs of college tuition, textbooks, and fewer careers available to support college graduates, college graduates find themselves working at the same low-paying jobs as those who did not go to college. Meanwhile, the college graduate has a difficult time advancing economically because the college loans do not come without the attachment of very high interest rates. College tuition continues to rise, as does the interest rates on college loans, even when other interest rates have been on the decline.[35]

Attacking our educational system in these ways prevents our children and any future generations from becoming self-actualized, critical thinking adults. Reducing our ability to think critically is also being attacked at the DNA level, by causing harm to the health and well-being of the population, which also impairs overall cognitive function. This is being done through the use of chemicals in our food such as using unnecessary pesticides, artificial sweeteners and additives. It is being done by adding fluoride to our drinking water. It is being done by exposing children to heavy metals by increasing the number of vaccines being used that contain aluminum or thimerosal, a mercury-containing compound. It is being done by adding pollutants to the air through geo engineering (chemtrails). It is also being done by manufacturing and requiring the use of GMO (Genetically Modified Organisms) seeds by farmers, which are known to hold less nutritional value than seeds that are not genetically modified.

Knowledge is power. As more people become aware that their feelings of powerlessness have been part of a socially conditioned agenda and this is not a natural part of the human condition, then fewer people will choose to side with this negativity, giving their power away. It is as simple as remembering our connection to one another, and that above all else, we are unified through a collective consciousness, linking us through our hearts to a greater mind. We are not less than any other person on this planet and no one is born defective. We do not need to work on ourselves in order to be lovable or loved, complete and whole. We do not need to be fixed. This is the lie that we have been led to believe. However, individuals are starting to take back their power by not being afraid to ask questions when things do not make sense. When the majority of us learn to rely on ourselves to uncover the truth instead of accepting whatever answer is being given, then there will be a great shift in the collective consciousness. The Internet has been a powerful tool for people to do their own research and find out their own truth. Like-minded people are coming together through social networks and the Internet has also provided people with ways to find alternative news sources, encouraging people to think critically.

Spiritual Disempowerment

Aside from the attack on our mental well-being, we have also been attacked spiritually. Ancient spiritual teachings and wisdom was replaced with indoctrinated religious ideologies, leading to what we know today as "organized religion". When we become familiar with tribal societies, their way of life, and their spiritual practices, we can see that the moment rulers conquered the land and demanded that the people of the land change their ways, a spiritual breakdown occurred at this same time.

Rather than fostering our natural ability to connect with the spiritual part of ourselves, we have been taught that spirituality occurs *outside of us* and that we are separate from the divine – that spirituality is something we must strive for, because it is always slightly out of reach. We are led to believe that we must rely on religious institutions to provide us with our spiritual lessons and practices, and the clergy or the church holds the solution to our salvation. We are shown how to pray and what songs we should sing. We are told that we are born as sinners and the only way to resolve our shortcomings is to follow a set of rules according to the clergy's interpretation. Negative emotions such as fear and guilt are preferred emotional response, which is how people become manipulated and controlled through religion.

In order for any religious group to form a community, they instill separatism. The belief that my God is better than your God or that certain people or behaviors are considered sinful while others are acceptable, perpetuates hate and separatism, and this is how one begins to identify oneself. The ego forms an identity that associates the ideal self as being a Jew, a Christian, or a Muslim, for example, as opposed to recognizing one's individual uniqueness as being the acceptable self. Religions thrive by convincing people that their original, true self is flawed, so an artificial self is necessary to replace the true self.

The artificial self is formed out of a set of principles that are linked to the religious group's ideology instead of embracing and loving ourselves just the way we are. However, real spiritual growth happens when we embrace ourselves and love ourselves as fully as we can, just as we are. We cannot evolve spiritually if we believe we have a diminished sense of self or if we believe we are lacking in any way. If we believe we are flawed or powerless to change anything in our lives, then this is what will be our experience. Religious institutions, by design, have lead people away from their natural connection to oneness, with the idea that we are born powerless, unworthy, imperfect, and in need of saving.

Today, there are greater opportunities for people to rediscover and reconnect with their spirit. This is happening as more people are turning to yoga, meditation, the new age movement, and naturopathic treatments. Participating in these types of things as opposed to following religious teachings can help us rediscover ways that we can authentically love ourselves as a perfect part of creation, rather than accepting that we are less than creation or separate from it. We do not have to change ourselves or buy into the belief that we are flawed and imperfect in order to give and receive love. We are made out of love and we already vibrate as a being of love.

Emotional Disempowerment

The third way that our power has been attacked is emotionally and this is done through the money system. We are hindered emotionally whenever we place a monetary value on things necessary for our survival such as housing, food, health, and transportation. We measure our own worth as merely a working citizen, instead of remembering the true nature of who we really are. We cannot realize our true self when we are constantly measuring our own worth and value by a materialistic meter stick.

We will never have enough, because there is always another commercial reminding us that we need more, or that the things we have are too old or not good enough. There will always be someone else who will have more wealth, more money, and more resources. If we measure our worth by these things, we will start to believe that there is something fundamentally wrong with us, because we never seem to have enough money or possessions. Many of us live in constant fear for our survival, especially if we lose our job or see our loved ones lose theirs. Most of us are told, and believe, that we are not more than a few paychecks away from losing our home, having our car repossessed, or we may feel forced to eat a diet that isn't as healthy as we desire, simply because we can only stretch our money so far.

We drive to our job in order to pay for the car we need to get there, and we leave our house empty all day just so we will be able to make enough money to afford to sleep in it at the end of our long workday. We are emotionally drained by a money system that is supposed to sustain us. We are tired, bored, stressed and apathetic, but our survival depends on living this way, day after day. We trade our time, our passion, and our life for money. The money trap enslaves us, because those who control the money supply will always rule over those who do not.

The Federal Reserve gives the false impression that they are part of the government or managed and overseen by the government, but this is not true. They purposely use the word "Federal" in their name in order to deceive the public that they have government oversight when in fact, they do not. Contrary to the vague claims published on the Federal Reserve website that they are "not 'owned' by anyone" or that they are "not a private, profit-making institution", they do state that they are "independent within the government" and that The Federal Reserve "is considered an independent central bank". There are "12 regional Federal Reserve Banks" that make up the Federal Reserve, and since 100% of its shareholders are private banks, then by definition, this can be nothing other than a private enterprise that is managed by the wealthiest banking cartels in the world.[36]

Federal Reserve Notes accounts for a guaranteed 6% return to banking shareholders. "In addition to this guaranteed 6% return, the banks get interest from the taxpayers on their 'reserves'. The basic reserve requirement set by the Federal Reserve is 10%. The website of the Federal Reserve Bank of New York explains that as money is re-deposited and reloaded throughout the banking system. This 10% held in 'reserve' can be fanned into ten times that sum in loans; that is, $10,000 in reserves becomes $100,000 in loans. Among other special benefits, banks and other financial institutions can borrow at the low Fed funds rate of about 2%. They can then turn around and put this money into 30-year Treasury bonds at 4.5%, earning an immediate 2.5% from the taxpayers, just by virtue of their position as favored banks."[37]

Wright Patman, Chairman of the House Banking and Currency Committee in the 1960s, called the Federal Reserve "a total money-making machine." He wrote: "When the Federal Reserve writes a check for a government bond it does exactly what any bank does, it creates money. It created money simply by writing a check."[36]

What is worse is that there is no government or citizen's oversight over The Federal Reserve. In 2007, PBS Journalist, Jim Lehrer interviewed Alan Greenspan, Chairman of the Federal Reserve from 1987 to 2006. Greenspan said, "The Federal Reserve is an independent agency, and that means, basically, that there is no other agency of government which can overrule actions that we take."[38] For those who have tried to challenge The Federal Reserve, things have not turned out favorably.

On June 4, 1963, a virtually unknown Presidential decree, Executive Order 11110, was signed with the authority to basically strip the Bank of its power to loan money to the United States Federal Government with interest. With the stroke of a pen, President Kennedy declared that the privately owned Federal Reserve Bank would soon be out of business. We all know this ended badly with his assassination, and the banking cartels continued with their business as usual.[39]

Knowledge Of Oneness Is Taking Back Your Power

Knowledge is power. Once we become aware that there has been an agenda to take power away from the people by dumbing us down, and by keeping us enslaved and diseased at every level – mentally, emotionally, spiritually and physically, then we can find our way out of this entrapment and rediscover the truth. The first step is to become aware that this has been done purposefully and maliciously through the establishment of these artificial matrixes.

We have been taught that we are separate from one another and we therefore must compete for survival. We are conditioned to believe that we are innately flawed, so we adapt to a false identity that we think will be more accepted by others. We silence our voices out of fear that we will be ridiculed or rejected if we go against the status quo. We live in a world where we don't fully trust one another, where we think we are not good enough or that others are not good enough, because we accept and believe what we have been taught, even if things don't make sense. We continue to believe what we are told, because this is how we have been conditioned.

Once we shift the beliefs about ourselves and realize that we exhibit the same powerful characteristics and abilities as the intelligence that created us, and that our reality is the manifestation of what we choose to believe, we will be able to take our power back. We will be able to lift the curtain and realize that the controlling patterns in any population stems from "believing" that we can be controlled. No one can be controlled unless they believe in this possibility. When you know that you are equally powerful and valuable when you compare yourself to anything and anyone else, because you are ONE with All That Is, then you will know that there is no such thing as being *more than* or *less than*. Everything is equal, because everything is part of creation. It is the *belief* in separatism that brings about the imbalances we experience. The best way to overcome any controlling agenda is to stop believing that it has any control over you. Live your life as someone who is unified, loved, and whole. You are good enough just as you are, exactly as you have been created.

The act of controlling another person and the act of being controlled is always a two-way choice. You cannot be controlled or manipulated if you know that you are not controllable. Only those who feel separate or less than another can be controlled. When you know you are equal and deserving of all that life has to offer, that the universe will always provide, and that you are always connected to one truth, then you can never be controlled by anyone.

It is impossible to experience separatism and oneness at the same time. Remind yourself that you are wholeness expressed as a fractal and you are always connected to a larger cosmic mind.

Invite every positive thought that enters your mind to remain there and become part of your truth. Allow your heart to feel and experience the greatest joy, the deepest compassion, and the greatest connection to others. Do not allow your negative ego to try to talk you out of being the happiest person you can be. Do not allow limited beliefs to enter your mind. You don't have to set a time limit on how long you wish to remain in a positive state. You have the choice and the capacity to remain in a pure state of joy for the rest of your life and in every single moment that you exist, if this is the reality you want to experience.

We have all experienced difficult times at some point in our lives such as relationship struggles, financial hardships, illnesses, and loss. As we move through painful and unpleasant experiences, we often look back on those times and realize that it was through our hardships that the greatest growth occurred.

During times of darkness, when we reach our lowest point, we will eventually decide that our pain is too much to bear, and then we will make a change. It is those changes within our beliefs and thoughts that bring about our healing. The circumstances in our life do not heal us. We heal ourselves.

The idea that time heals all wounds has nothing to do with time. The reason that healing occurs gradually over the course of time is because it takes time for us to decide when we're ready to make a change in our beliefs and in our perceptions. This is what leads to our healing. However, we don't have to wait for time to pass in order to heal our wounds. We can heal anything we want in an instant, because there is no time other than the time of now. Our belief that healing takes a long time means that we are simply choosing to take time before we are ready to forgive, let go, and heal. True healing is nothing other than a shift in awareness and setting your intention that you are ready to be healed.

By deciding to place your focus on your connection to All That Is, and on what is whole rather than on what is separate, you will begin to see there is a flame of light that exists in all things. That which we perceive as being bad cannot affect us when we know that we are all one with All That Is.

Each one of us is contributing to the wholeness. This is the nature of who we truly are. Young children will remind us of this truth and so will everything in nature. You are not separate from the perceived good or the bad, because both are necessary in order to discover who you truly are. You can use your free will to choose the types of thoughts you wish to entertain – and what you focus on is what has led to all the incremental changes that have occurred throughout your life, leading you to this very moment where you are today.

CHAPTER THREE

YOU ARE NOT THE EGO

Dear One,

There are many things to discover; about yourself, about your life and about the universe. What I want to share with you will help you live a richer, more abundant life. This is not simply in terms of monetary abundance, but this is the abundance of unlimited possibilities that exist all around you.

Many of you have not been encouraged to listen to your intuition and follow your heart, yet once you do this, you will be able to access a deeper wisdom of knowing who you are and what your life's purpose is all about. The critical and destructive voice of the ego has been the dominant voice inside your head and it drowns out the sound of my voice.

Your ego tries to label everything. It believes that 'the infinite' must be contained or categorized by clear definitions, but 'the infinite' can never be contained or simplified. Energy is consciousness and consciousness is energy. Because you are a being of conscious, infinite energy, there are no labels that could possibly define you. You just are.

I've been called God, Great Spirit, The Christ Consciousness, The Creator, The Source, Allah, Lord, Jehovah, and other names that identify me as a deity. You wish to call me, "The Voice of Creation" for the purpose of delivering this information into a book. However, a label cannot define me anymore than a label can define you. Anytime you confine me with a name or pin me to a religious group, you are putting a limited constraint on ALL that I am and ALL that I am trying to help you become.

As difficult as this might be to comprehend... I am you and you are me. Everything is all part of the one. This means that you exist in everything and everything exists in you. There is no real separation. You only have the illusion that you are separate, and your ego has perpetuated this belief causing you to see through a lens that makes it seem like there is duality, difficulties, and differentiation. Every perceived experience is labeled by the ego, but you always have the free will to choose and become all that you can be within the embodiment of All That Is.

The Voice of Creation exists in all things. It is the soft, still voice that lies at the core of your being – that is guiding you through all your life experiences. You will discover the work you came here to do simply by honing in on this voice within. Listening and allowing passionate excitement to come through your heart in everything you do and knowing that everything will always turn out exactly as it should, are the key components for aligning with your authentic self.

When you remember that you are ONE with All That Is, and not separate from the one that created you, you will be able to receive communication from more evolved beings that can guide you along your journey towards ascension. Your higher self, your guardians, your God-Self and all the ascended masters are always within your reach and they are here to help you with anything you need.

When operating at the level of unity consciousness, you will find that these beings are just more evolved aspects of you, because everything is all one. Your free will determines whether you will choose to listen to your ego's voice and believe in the illusion of separation, or whether you will listen to the voice of higher consciousness, which links you to All That Is.

As you read through this chapter, you will begin to identify and become more conscious of your ego's voice and the interference it has had in your ascension and connection to All That Is. You can learn to live side-by-side with your ego without allowing it to take over the driver's seat. This chapter will show you how.

Thank you for giving this monumental awakening a chance to work in your life. A shift has occurred within the universal consciousness of humanity and you get to be part of it. The time is now. A new wave of light, enlightenment, higher consciousness, and joy has emerged on your planet, making this shift possible. Please join me now in this next chapter in your life.

Transcribed From:
The Voice of Creation

. . . .

"The authentic self is the best part of a human being. It's the part of you that already cares that is already passionate about evolution. When your authentic self miraculously awakens and becomes stronger than your ego, then you will truly begin to make a difference in this world. You will literally enter into a partnership with the creative principle." *– Andrew Cohen*

You are not your ego. Your ego is nothing more than your brain's attempt to try to identify and understand the self. The ego is the mechanical part of the brain, operating much like a computer that regurgitates old programs and reinforces existing habits, but this is not your authentic self.

Your authentic self is energetic and non-physical. The real you can be described as an infinite and immortal soul that is made up of the energetic frequency of love, which expands into multiple dimensions. As a multidimensional being, your authentic self cannot be contained within the ego's limited labels of self.

The ego is the illusionary self, or the brain's attempt to understand what the self is. It is the brain's job to label and compartmentalize everything in order to make sense of the physical world, and this includes applying labels to the self.

Your mind is filled with labels. Beliefs have been formed about who you think you are by the named characteristics your ego has assigned you. You might call yourself introverted or extroverted, good at certain tasks and bad at others, rich or poor, selfish or giving, superior or inferior, fearful or courageous, challenged or bored.

Your ego is your brain's artificial construct of who you think you are, but this is not the real you, because if you were to change or discard all of the labels, you would still exist. The labels did not create your existence so how can labels define your existence?

Everything gets labeled, critiqued, and judged by the ego, and sometimes quite harshly. Because this is the nature of the ego, it can never experience fulfillment, peace, or satisfaction. It is like a cup with a hole at the bottom that continues to run dry and needs to be filled constantly. In order to feel worthy and fulfilled, the ego seeks to be surrounded by material possessions or things that are labeled as fulfilling. However, the ego can never achieve genuine fulfillment when it's constantly judging and measuring its value against something else, or comparing what it has with what it doesn't have.

The good news is you are not your ego. Your ego's labels can never taint your authentic self and you always get to decide whether to allow your ego to be the driver or not. You can simply "observe" the ego's constructed labels, judgments, and any negative thoughts that arise, rather than "react" to the ego. This puts you in the drivers seat and then you can parent your ego instead of being subservient to it. You would never allow a small child to drive you around in a car. Therefore, why should you allow your ego to be the dictator in your life, driving you around recklessly where you don't want to go?

When you came into this world as a small infant, your ego started growing and developing along with you. When you first began to experience hunger, pain, or any type of discomfort, your ego began to take shape. If you were responded to with love and acceptance, your ego began writing programs that ascribed positive labels to the self. However, it was not humanly possible for your parents to meet every emotional and physical need with perfect satisfaction. There were shortcomings along the way, because there were times when you experienced disappointment. There were times when your needs were dealt with impatiently by caregivers or parents. Your ego applied positive or negative labels to the self from every experience, based on the interpretation of how others responded and reacted to you.

Since the ego believes it is separate from everything, applying labels helps provide predicable and familiar definitions to a world that otherwise appears chaotic and random. This is why beliefs about past experiences are carried over to define new experiences, even though new experiences are unrelated to the past.

Our true self knows its connection to All That Is. The true self does not have a need to label or judge anything negatively, because there is nothing to fear when we know we are connected to All That Is.

When we allow ego-interpreted labels to paint our reality and guide us in the decisions we make, we will find that our decisions are not reflective of the highest and greatest good for ourselves or for others. Ego-based decision-making has been destructive to our current ways of existence.

As a society, our egos have been our rulers and since the ego interprets everything as separate, it does not pay attention to any universal free will principles, such as the idea to "live and let live", which would be honoring another's free will. Free will violations are the reason why we see power struggles among governments and citizens, why domestic violence and child abuse occurs in families, and why there is discrimination within societies.

The ego believes it has a duty to shape and mold other people, the planet, and nature – all according to the ego's label of itself within the world. Arrogance and self-righteousness have led to behaviors that justify having power and control over others and this is what has caused so much destruction and the killing off of life on the planet.

Once individuals become aware that living according to the ego is a choice, then we will begin to see a shift collectively as well as individually. We can co-exist in a world where there are no more wars, tyranny, genocide, and crimes against nature. Greed, selfishness, and self-righteousness are direct constructs of the ego. If you believe in the labels constructed by the ego mind, then everyday is going to be a battle. It is always going to be you against the world rather than enjoying your wholeness within the body of creation.

Once you identify your ego's labels and become the 'observer of your ego' instead of allowing your ego to 'observe and dominate you', you will take back your power and live according to the way you have been designed. You can live side-by-side with your ego instead of allowing it to be in charge.

Shifting Out Of Ego-Based Thought Towards Cardio Intelligence Or Heart Centered Thinking

While ego-based thought is centered in the brain, there is another way of thinking that comes from the heart or from the higher self. This is called Heart Centered Thinking or Cardio Intelligence. This is a real method of thinking and it involves the communication of information that passes through the heart.

This type of communication and mode of thought was well known by our ancient ancestors, who understood the heart to be more than an organ that pumps blood. Today, scientists are proving that our heart *thinks* and *communicates*.[40]

Research findings from The Institute of HeartMath provide an insight into the human heart's communication systems. In 1991, Neurocardiologist Dr. J. Andrew Armour introduced the term "heart brain." He observed that the heart possesses a complex and intrinsic nervous system that is comprised of a network of more than 40,000 neurons. The heart secretes hormones and neurotransmitters, it senses and processes information, assists with making decisions, and the heart has demonstrated the ability to learn and remember information, very much like the brain.[40]

In utero, the heart begins to beat before the brain is completely formed. There is no separate brain that exists to tell your heart to begin beating. Your heart simply beats on its own, and this same thing occurs during heart transplant operations. At no point in time does the heart need to be connected to a separate brain in order for it to function. The heart actually sends more signals to the brain than the brain sends to the heart.[41]

The electrical component of the heart's electromagnetic field is about 60 times greater in amplitude than the brain. This magnetic field extends several feet away from the body and has been shown to contribute to the magnetic attractions or repulsions between individuals, effecting social exchanges and relationships.[42]

Science has also shown that the heart cells from multiple people and even between animals and people will beat in unison when placed together in a petri dish. However, when scientists place brain cells together, no synchronized communication occurs, and instead, the brain cells perish.[43]

It has also been found that the rhythmic beating patterns of the heart change significantly as we experience different emotions. Negative emotions, such as hostility, anxiety, or frustration, are associated with an erratic, disordered, incoherent pattern in the heart's rhythm. In contrast, positive emotions such as love or appreciation are associated with smooth, ordered, coherent patterns in the heart's rhythmic activity. The changes in the heart's beating patterns create corresponding changes in the structure of the electromagnetic field radiated by the heart, measured by a technique called spectral analysis.[41]

When the heart's rhythm is coherent, the brain and body will experience a number of positive benefits such as better health, greater mental clarity, intuitive abilities, and better decision-making. This provides further scientific evidence that there is a heart-mind connection. Positive attitudes and feelings clearly determine the state of our total health and this has always been communicated from the heart.[42]

Heart-based thought connects you to the ebb and flow of universal consciousness. When you follow your intuition and give attention to positive feelings, feel passionate about your life, and fall in love with the universe you live in, you will automatically be operating from your heart and not from your ego.

We all know what the energy of love feels like and this feeling is always experienced in the heart. Likewise, pain, sorrow and grief are also felt in the heart, which gives rise to the condition of "having a broken heart". Whatever emotions you feel and anytime you experience intuitive thought, express creativity, and experience the feeling of connection to others or identify with the beauty in nature, your experience is always felt and expressed in the heart. Science can now explain that heartfelt emotions are the result of your heart's ability to think, interact, and transmit information through the electromagnetic field that surrounds it.

With every beat of your heart, you are transmitting a vibratory frequency that carries and sends waves of information out through the magnetic field that surrounds your body. Everything responds to this frequency – your body, your brain, other people, as well as a higher universal mind.

You are in constant communication with everything in the universe simply because you are a sentient being. Just like your body, the earth also has a magnetic field surrounding it. What you think and feel is transmitted through an interconnecting electromagnetic grid, and this grid is connected to everything in the entire universe.

When you let go of the ego's interference, you will release limited beliefs and the idea that you are separate from the universe or that the universe is working against you. When your ego is not engaged and directing your life, your heart can open its communication to you because it is linked electromagnetically to the universe that you are part of. The ability to solve problems and discover creative solutions, experience peace even during the most stressful times, find love, and gain insights, happens whenever we rely on Cardio Intelligence.

Meditation To Quiet The Ego-Mind

There is a meditative exercise I enjoy doing, which helps quiet the chatter of the ego mind. I simply gaze at a tree, but this is not a typical way of seeing a tree. It is *the way* I gaze at the tree.

I often do this exercise when I go to the grocery store. Before I walk inside the store, I take a few moments in the parking lot while still sitting in the car and I find a nearby tree to gaze at. You can also do this exercise while sitting on a park bench or even while gazing out your window from home. It is a simple but powerful meditation that only takes a few minutes.

As I gaze at the tree, it is as though it is not called a tree. It has no label or name. It just is. During this time, I don't attach any concepts about what the tree means to me. I don't think about the changing seasons or how the tree is affected by the seasons. I don't think about whether the tree has leaves or not, whether the tree is skinny, tall, short, or broad. I simply look and observe this beautiful thing before me with no name.

My eyes blur slightly as I take in its form, shape, and colors, but I do this without analyzing what I am seeing. By removing any identification of the tree, I begin to experience the tree's 'is-ness' instead of the labels associated with it. I begin to notice that the tree is energy in its purest form. All that is left without labels is a source of energy that I can connect to. There are no words. No labels. Only a connection felt deep within the heart.

When you practice this exercise, it will become apparent that everything perceived in physical reality has been characterized by a multitude of ego-defined labels. When your ego-mind labels and categorizes things, it limits your ability to connect to what is real, because you will observe the world only in the ways your ego has labeled it.

During the spring, a tree begins to bud leaves and flowers. Birds, spiders, and other small creatures find that the tree is a nice place to nest. Depending on how you label this, you might find the critters to be beautiful aspects of nature or you may find that nest building and spiders are messy, intrusive, and annoying.

To a logger or developer, the tree represents a commodity. To a farmer, the tree might be viewed as productive or not productive. If it is a fruit-bearing tree, it could either be a prolific year or not a prolific year. The tree cannot be perceived for all that it is once it becomes labeled. The moment we label our experience, we limit and confine it, and perceive it as less than what it truly is.

You will notice the fullest potential and most authentic beauty in everything the moment you quiet the ego's need to label. Accepting ego-constructed labels to define reality is what results in all of the negative behaviors that have plagued our society. Self-righteousness, hatred towards the self and others, addiction, violence, discrimination, prejudices, and greed, are all behaviors derived from the ego's fixation on labels.

The ego identifies with all things separate, so it focuses on things like fear, lack, and scarcity. Once we are aware that there are two ways we can experience thought, we can shift into heart-based, Cardio Intelligence instead, which is positive, loving and expansive.

We can 'observe' the attitudes and beliefs derived from the ego instead of 'responding' to them. We can choose different attitudes and beliefs that are more in alignment with our intentions and what we prefer instead of what we do not prefer. We can replace worry with peace, bitterness with love, and constriction with expansion. We can choose to open our heart, which is "The Link" to the energetic field that connects us to a greater cosmic consciousness. We are always connected to this field, but we aren't always aware when the ego mind has its grip on our focus.

Attitudes and Beliefs

No matter what situation we find ourselves in, there are just two core beliefs and attitudes from which we choose:

> 1.) I am a victim of my experience, which is ego-centered thinking.

> 2.) I am an active participant; or a co-creator of my experience, which is heart centered thinking.

The victim's perspective is always lacking, always wanting, never having, and does not seek solutions. Nothing is ever good enough for the victim and the victim lives in a constant state of hopelessness, fear, and despair. It is always someone else's fault that the victim's needs are not met. This all stems from the ego, portraying a very limited perspective of reality.

The active participant on the other hand, operates as a co-creator, seeking love, patience, openness, acceptance, and faith in what is good. The active participant seeks solutions to problems and does not give in to despair. This attitude keeps the heart open, and when the heart is open, the reality you experience will no longer appear to be limited and debilitating. Instead, you will enter the field to higher consciousness where you will link to an infinite stream of creativity and abundance. You will find solutions to your problems and you will discover that you are connected to an endless stream of expansive, creative potentialities, just waiting to be realized.

If you feel like nothing is going your way, you are most likely operating from a victim stance. We all shift in and out of these moments, where at times we decide to play the victim role and other times we will shift back into having a more positive attitude. Most of us operate like we are playing a game of Ping-Pong. We don't always remember that we are the one in charge of our beliefs and attitudes, so we bounce around from having negative thoughts and feelings to having positive thoughts and feelings. We have highs and lows and our ego often convinces us that life is happening to us, when in reality, we are the observer and perceiver, applying the meanings we choose for every experience.

We can allow our ego to label our experiences negatively by rehashing the idea that we are separate, or we can simply 'observe' the labels and decide not to give them any merit. If something does not bring you joy, or aid in the well-being of yourself and others, you can choose a position of neutrality, and simply observe the ego's labels instead of acting and responding to them.

It is important to pay attention to the chatter that goes on in the mind. It can be so subtle that you will barely notice it's there. You can become an observer of your thoughts by keeping a piece of paper with you throughout the day and whenever you catch yourself having a negative thought, jot it down. You may need to do this over the course of several days, because it can take time to learn how to listen to what's really going on inside your head.

Once you notice the mind chatter and all the ways you have been labeling your experiences, you will be amazed at all the negative thoughts you have been allowing your ego to feed you. It will begin to make more sense why you have been feeling tired, depressed, or stressed. Your own thoughts might be toxic, blocking you from your true potential.

Once you have compiled a list of the negative thoughts causing you to feel constricted, unhappy, or unworthy, you can write down loving, kind, thoughts in their place. The positive thoughts and feelings can become your affirmations, and you can refer to your revised list the next time you become aware of negative mind-chatter.

At first, it may not feel natural to believe in the positive affirmations; however reading from your list on a regular basis is necessary to replace the old programming. Eventually, you won't need to refer to your list anymore. Positive thoughts will become second nature the more you practice this.

How Positive Thoughts Helped Me Lose Weight

I was approximately 70 pounds overweight, which I gained over a period of about 7 years. I could not understand why the weight was not coming off. I joined a gym, walked as often as possible, and ate more vegetables. Nothing seemed to work until I started to pay attention to what I was telling myself.

I found that my core belief was: "No matter how hard I try, I am never going to lose this weight. There must be something wrong with me."

I was convinced that something was the matter with me, so I had blood work done to have my thyroid checked, only to discover there was no physical reason why I kept holding onto the excess weight. The culprit was actually my attitude. Since I believed I would never lose weight, that was exactly what I continued to manifest.

I broke this negative cycle when I joined an online weight loss club that provided software to track everything I ate. The online community support was very positive and this positive energy seemed to rub off on me.

For the first time, I began to understand the reasons why I gained excess weight in the first place. A pattern of negative thoughts triggered an emotional eating response and eating for emotional reasons became a habit. I ate every time I felt sad, angry, anxious, or emotionally empty. I was using food to eliminate unpleasant feelings, but the unpleasant feelings continued to surface because I wasn't doing anything about the headful of negative thoughts and negative labels that colored my reality.

Once I started networking with other people who publically shared their struggles and successes with weight loss, I began to feel hopeful. My negative beliefs about my weight started to shift and become more positive. When I felt like eating for emotional reasons, I decided to take a walk instead. Changing this one behavior caused my endorphins to increase, because I increased the amount of exercise I was getting. This helped bring about a better mood, making it even easier to "choose my attitude". By inviting more positive thoughts into my mind, positive emotions followed, and just like magic, the weight started to fall off.

After I lost a couple of pounds, I felt even more inspired. I started telling myself, "I really can lose weight. I am just like everyone else trying to lose weight. There is nothing wrong with me. I REALLY CAN DO THIS." The fundamental change in *my beliefs* about losing weight led to my actual weight loss.

A sense of accomplishment and personal empowerment swept through me as I let go of the ego's need to label my experiences in a negative way. Cardio Intelligence emerged. My heart and mind became filled with infinite possibilities, and it became easier to maintain a positive belief about my ability to lose weight. Instead of feeling like a helpless victim, I was in charge of my own destiny. I lost weight because my attitude about my ability to lose weight changed.

You Have The Power To Create The Change You Want

Once you replace negative beliefs with positive beliefs, remove the victim label, and stop believing that you are limited according to your ego, you can bring forth any intention you want to manifest. When you engage your heart by expressing loving thoughts and feelings for yourself and others, your ego has to step aside. It can no longer serve as the dictator in your life. Instead, your heart's consciousness or your Cardio Intelligence serves as the link, connecting you to other people and to a universal cosmic consciousness.

We live in a "YES" universe. When you desire to make a change and you simply believe it can be done, you can count on the universe to take it from there. You will be amazed at what you can accomplish and manifest with positive thoughts and emotions. The mere desire to change your attitude from negative to positive will instantly engage your heart. Once you engage your heart and focus your intention, you will simultaneously engage the larger universal mind to move through you and empower you.

Anything you are unhappy with or that you want to change can be changed if you truly desire this and feel it at the heart level. You are a co-creator within a greater universal mind. You are always connected to this. It is simply a matter of deciding to align with it.

If you don't like some aspect of yourself or what is happening with your life, you have the power and the ability to change it. For example, if you have identified yourself as poor, disabled, widowed, sick, or old, you can choose how the labels will affect you or won't affect you. What you tell yourself and what you believe to be a limitation is the only limitation that exists. Once you strip away any negative labels, you are left with infinite possibilities and potential.

It is common to feel trapped by the belief that there are some things you cannot change such as your age, your physical limitations, or health conditions. However, your perception of your age, your perception of your physical limitations, and your perception of your health, is what gives those things their meaning. It is not the number of years old that you are that determines your age. Your perception of your age or the perception of how your disability impacts your life is what brings forth the character of your experience. You characterize your experiences. What you define as a disability could actually be a prodigy or a gift to humanity, simply by changing the definition of the label.

There are children diagnosed with autism who use parts of their brain unlike their peers, and they express talents and abilities that could not be brought forth if it wasn't for their so-called "disability". Medical experts and educators use words of limitation such as, "disability" or "disease" to define a person or a person's condition.

A label can never define a person or any person's abilities. Only the spirit within the person can define a person and there are no words in the dictionary that can define anybody. Every person is unique and every person has the capability to lead a life that is filled with infinite potential and possibilities. Our infinite existence and unlimited potential is who we truly are. We are not merely the construct of a bunch of labels set forth by the ego mind.

When you catch yourself having victimizing thoughts, simply chose to identify with the opposite, which will open your heart to receive information from a greater universal mind. Remember that every thought and belief you have is a choice. You can choose to have thoughts and identify yourself as being a victim or you can chose to have thoughts as an empowered co-creator. You are choosing between ego-centered and heart centered thinking all the time, whether you are conscious of this or not.

Below are some examples of thoughts we all experience from

time to time, so you can see the difference in the two modes of thought. At any time, we can play the victim role or we can play the role of the co-creator.

Victim - "This relationship is never going to work."
Co-Creator - "This relationship will work because I will do my part to try to make things better and I will focus on my partner's good qualities."

Victim - "How am I ever going to pay these bills?"
Co-Creator - "I will always find a way to pay the bills. The universe always provides. I am thankful for all the abundance I have."

Victim - "I am sick and tired that I never seem to feel any better."
Co-Creator - "My body knows how to heal itself. My mind and body are one and I have the power to align my thoughts and body in positive ways for optimum health and well-being."

Victim - "I can't believe I did something so stupid."
Co-Creator - "Everyone learns by making mistakes. I am intelligent and capable of learning and growing from every experience."

Victim - "I don't have time."
Co-Creator - "I am the director of my own time. I will give myself the appropriate amount of time I need to achieve anything I want."

We can "observe" negative thoughts as opposed to reacting to them, and we can change our definitions so that our labels and beliefs are more positive. A third option is we can take a neutral stand. Taking a neutral stand and choosing not to label situations or individuals as neither positive or negative brings us towards an even higher state of consciousness, called forgiveness and surrender.

Forgiveness and Surrender - How And Why We Should Forgive, Especially When Bad Things Happen To Good People

"But I say to you, Love your enemies and pray for those who persecute you."
– *Matthew 5:44*

Scholars, prophets, religious teachings, and spiritual masters have taught the importance of forgiveness. We have been told that if we truly forgive those who have wronged us, we will be set free. While this is true, most people see forgiveness as something that is conditional and dependent on many factors.

When we examine our criminal justice system, an offender's level of prosecution will depend on the agreed-upon level of the offense, which has been written into laws we are expected to follow. For example, a person who is driving too fast will get a speeding ticket, while a serial killer will likely face the death penalty, or at least, life in prison. Most people practice forgiveness the same way our society practices law. After all, in order for everything to be fair and just, it is easier to forgive someone who accidentally hurt your feelings than to forgive someone who murdered your grandmother.

We tend to withhold forgiveness and hold onto resentments because this provides us with a false belief that we are operating from a moral high ground. We want to maintain a fair and balanced system and we believe we are doing the right thing when we feel resentment and anger towards the person who committed the atrocities we are faced with.

We hold onto these resentments with great passion in order to feel that there is justice in the world. We presume that our resentments will somehow successfully punish the one who offended us. We become the judge of our own internal justice system. But whom are we really judging? Who are we really punishing?

Studies show that our mental state and our attitudes affect our overall physical health. One in three people who have cancer also have anxiety or other mental health challenges.[44] Holding onto anger and resentment can wreck havoc on our health and well-being. There is plenty of research to support how negative emotions can facilitate an environment in the body where cancer cells can grow; whereas a mind that is positive can heal tumors and foster an environment where cancer cannot thrive.[45] What we think and feel affects our body and our overall health.

We all know that holding onto resentment is not good for us, but what do we do? How can we help ourselves feel better when someone has hurt us to the core and been so unjust? How can we forgive someone who burglarized our home and took every one of our possessions, including things that have sentimental value, which cannot be replaced? Or worse, how can we forgive someone who tortured, raped, or killed one of our children? Can we forgive someone who chose to drink and drive, taking the innocent lives of a mother and her small children?

To consider forgiving such inhumane acts used to disturb me to the core. Acting in accordance with forgiveness is almost as calloused and insane as the person who committed the offense. To forgive someone and release all anger and judgment following such a horrific offense would mean you no longer hold any resentment towards the offending person. It means you have decided that you can move forward and be happy, no matter what the offender did, and no matter how awful the violation.

The act of forgiving feels as though you are surrendering your spirit to terrible atrocities, which can lead to more feelings of victimization. Yet, not being able to forgive leads to feelings of guilt and inner turmoil. This double edge sword has a negative outcome either way, whether you decide to forgive someone or not.

During my own awakening, I realized there was something seriously flawed with this spiritual teaching. We have been pushed into practicing forgiveness without knowing what real forgiveness is.

The true meaning of forgiveness means to give energy back to its original owner. When you feel sad, angry, or hurt by another person, it is because they dumped their negative emotions onto you, either through the words they expressed, or the actions they took.

Unknowingly, you took this energy that did not belong to you nor was it created by you. In order to "for-give", this energy must be given back to its owner.

Words do not need to be exchanged for true forgiveness to take place and for you to be freed from another person's negative energy. When you practice forgiveness by doing this next meditative exercise, you will learn how to transform negative energy into positive energy, turn darkness into light, and you will learn how to transmute energy back to its natural state. Everything begins as love and everything responds to love.

The most effective way to give back another person's energy is to first think about the emotions you experienced from the person's hurtful words or actions. Whether you feel angry, bitter, sad, spiteful, or unsettled, allow yourself to recognize all feelings as honorable and valid. You do not need to feel ashamed or disappointed for having strong feelings. Recognize the level of discomfort these feelings are causing.

Once you identify the emotions that have been holding you back, imagine that you are placing these unpleasant emotions into a box. The emotions can look like words written on a piece of paper or they can be represented as blobs of color. It does not matter how this looks to your imagination. Your mind will automatically provide you with the best imaginative expression or representation when you are doing this exercise.

As you place each of the negative emotions into a box, imagine that you are wrapping the box like a present. It is important that you make the present look pretty so you are wrapping up the feelings with love and kindness.

Then, imagine yourself handing the wrapped present back to the person who gave you the negative energy and say the following words, "Thank you for the experience you gave me; however, these negative emotions are not mine to own, so I am giving them back to you now."

When you do this, you are actually transforming negative energy into positive energy. Everything responds to the highest vibration of love, which is why you will always see results when you find ways to turn darkness into light, or animosity into love.

You can practice this forgiveness exercise any time you need, as often as you need, and with any number of people you feel you need to forgive. Most people feel the benefits of this imaginative exercise immediately after they do it.

Whenever we experience ethereal changes by engaging our imagination in new ways, we are creating the bridge for changes to take place on the physical plane. This is because everything that was ever brought into physical reality began as a thought. Everything started in the mind, even before it took action through the heart of intention. YOU ARE a receiver, transmitter, transformer, and co-creator of energy.

As energetic beings, we have the capacity to send and receive energy through our thoughts, emotions, and actions. When our thoughts and emotions harbor fear, sorrow, anger, and resentment, our life force energy changes in its density, so it won't flow as easily. Denser energies become lodged or trapped in the body, leading to disease and illness.

Acupuncturists understand this and work with meridians within the body to help release and remove these pockets of trapped energy. The word dis-ease, literally means without ease. The word e-motion, is energy in motion. If our emotions are negatively charged by our negative thoughts, this can create dis-ease within our physical body, or it can create dis-ease within our spiritual body, which is what leads to unresolved karma.

Holding onto resentment reinforces the ego's identification that the self is separate and alone. The ego's labels and the idea that the self is a victim becomes our physical experience. Forgiveness is a proven method for stepping completely out of the victim role and back into Cardio Intelligence where there are infinite possibilities.

Once we realize that we are all connected and linked to one another, because we are all one, we can come to the understanding that there is a bigger story unfolding in our life. Our experiences with others can provide us with important lessons we can take with us when it is our turn to leave this planet. Once we learn to see the bigger picture, and remember our oneness, the art of forgiveness becomes effortless and natural.

One way to see the bigger picture is to look at this from a rudimentary perspective or from a spectator's point of view, so you aren't emerged in the center of opposition. If you are a sports fan or have children who are active in sports, this next example illustrates how knowing your connection to others can lead you towards the path of forgiveness, making it easier to let go of resentment.

Seeing Oneness When There Is Opposition

My youngest son is very active in Taekwondo martial arts. At every tournament, my son and his opponent bow to one another and make eye contact before they begin to spar in their match. There is a common understanding that they are ONE of the same. They recognize that each individual is part of the martial arts community, respectfully working towards the same goal – which is to become better martial artists. The opponents also know that Taekwondo cannot exist and one cannot know his or her skill level, strengths, and weaknesses, until they pair up as opponents, competing against one another.

The challenge then begins in the form of a match. Sometimes one of the opponents gets hurt, and some matches are more difficult than others. Regardless of the outcome of "the match", the human spirit and the connection to their opponent remains stronger than anything else. At the end of the match, both opponents shake hands or hug one another, and this gesture is extended to the opponent's coach as well.

In real life, like in a Taekwondo tournament, we will experience opposition. With each opposition, we are given the same opportunities to learn from "the match" just like the martial artist does. Without seeing an opposing side, how can we clearly know who we are as an individual and what we stand for? Sometimes opposition helps us identify and solidify our values. Other times, opposition causes pain; but regardless of any circumstances, opposition forces us to make a choice about how we will respond when we feel resistance from another person. How will we play our part in the match? Will we respond according to our ego, by expressing anger and judgment? Instead, we can choose to react to any situation with openness, compassion, and love.

Sometimes our opponent will break rules. Rule breaking teaches us to clearly define what our own rules are. For example, if our feelings get hurt because of what someone said or did, it is important to be clear when we communicate "our rules" with our opponent in order to continue to play in that same match.

The primary rule that everyone must follow in a real life match is to respect our opponent. We can disagree respectfully by freely stating our needs and feelings without engaging the ego's emphasis on separatism. Respect is a heart-based trait, so whenever we are respectful towards our opponent, we will not engage the ego.

Since we define every life experience by our chosen perspectives, it is important to know that our decision to feel hurt or harmed by another person is a perception. Whenever we feel hurt by someone else, our brain opens its filing cabinet and retrieves all the previous experiences where similar hurts occurred in the past. Whatever has triggered us to feel hurt in a current situation often becomes categorized and labeled as being "painful" because our ego connects our current experience to a comparable experience from the past. When we believe we are victimized, we will react with a fight or flight response. In reality, we can only be a victim if we choose this as our label.

Sometimes we completely misunderstand another person. Our perceptions may be skewed when our brain compares our current experience with a past experience, and the two experiences are not actually related at all. The ego's labels of our experiences give us the illusion that we have had a similar experience in the past and therefore, we believe we need to have the same reactionary response that we used before.

In reality, everything is a separate experience and we always have a choice about how we will perceive and react to anything. Our past experiences and responses do not need to be re-experienced in the present unless we choose this.

When something that someone says or does causes you emotional pain, it is important to remember that your brain may have opened up its filing cabinet from the past in order to label your current situation as being one of pain and sorrow. You don't have to allow this to become your present experience however. We always have the ability to recreate the "now" so that it can be experienced any way we want. Every moment is brand new. Each moment of "now" is a new opportunity. We don't have to bring past labels or previously held beliefs into our present experience once we discover that this no longer serves us. We can choose new perspectives that stem from an entirely new awareness.

The next time you have a real life match or disagreement with another person, challenge yourself to handle your opponent differently. Ask yourself, "Am I attacking my opponent in the pursuit to prove I am right? Is my ego engaging in an 'I WON' attitude, or am I remembering that we are 'ALL ONE'? Am I being respectful towards my opponent and is my opponent being respectful towards me?

If your opponent is not being respectful towards you, the best way to gain respect from your opponent is to be respectful towards your opponent first. When you operate from a place of understanding and compassion towards the other person, no matter how different your views might be, your opponent will eventually mirror this back to you.

To get the most out of any disagreement, you can ask yourself, "What can I learn from my opponent?" There is always a bigger picture that holds the key for self-discovery when looking beyond the argument and remembering your connection to your opponent. Your opponent can provide you with the necessary reflection to show you how to heal and love yourself more fully. You will then stop seeing your opponent as the cause of your pain and suffering, but instead, your opponent is your teacher, aiding you in the process of personal growth and ascension. Those who oppose us are not really our enemies. They are our greatest teachers.

All matches or disagreements must come to an end. We have a choice about how we will handle opposition when we experience it. Will we embrace the lessons provided, or will we hold onto hostility and resentment like a poor sport? We can choose to feel grateful to our opponent for the lessons that opposition teaches us, which instantly shifts us out of the constraints of ego-centered thought and into Cardio Intelligence.

We will find that the universe is on our side as soon as we decide to stop siding with the ego's perception of pain, suffering, victimization, and resentment. When we remember we are connected to our opponent and not separate, it is easier to forgive and release resentment. We are all playing a part in ONE story called, "The Story of Humanity", and we are all doing this to the best of our abilities.

No matter how dark or challenging adversity appears, there is no challenge or opposition that can separate humanity from itself. We are all part of one humanity, sharing in the human experience, which is always felt at the heart-level, no matter how diverse we are in our beliefs, appearances, or personalities.

We are greater than any ego-defined labels of self. We are greater than our adversities. We are greater than the experiences we are having as physical beings. When we know that our true nature is expressed and felt in the heart, our ego will have no other option but to step aside.

CHAPTER FOUR

YOU ARE MULTIDIMENSIONAL EXISTING IN EVERYTHING, EVERYWHERE AT THE SAME TIME

Dear One,

You are a limitless being of infinite light because you are made of light. You are no less than me, for you are an exact replica of me. Your consciousness is omnipresent, which means you can exist in multiple places at the same time. Although you may only be aware of having a linear third and fourth dimensional existence, you actually exist as a multidimensional being, and this is how you are able to bring fourth dimensional manifestations into physical reality.

Whenever you perceive something, define what you believe to be true, and react to circumstances through your emotions, you are directing the vibrational output of your consciousness. As an energetic being, you are constantly radiating energy out into the universe. Your vibrational output is influenced by your perceptions and reactions, and this is based on the beliefs you carry with you.

Your energetic frequency will vibrate faster when your thoughts and feelings are positive, and it will vibrate slower when your thoughts and feeling are negative. The faster your consciousness is vibrating, the more familiar you will be with the multidimensional aspects of yourself because you will be able to transcend the time-space limitation of the third dimension. The only limitations are those created by the ego, which are the imaginary boundaries you have chosen to impose upon yourself, affecting your potential. Creation itself, is infinitely abundant and since you are part of creation, there are no boundaries in the universe or within the constructs of consciousness.

When viewing reality from a third dimensional perspective, it can be challenging to remove boundaries and limitations, but when you learn how to be the master over your thoughts and beliefs, higher dimensional versions of yourself will emerge, and you will come to know yourself as a multidimensional being. This chapter will acquaint you with your multidimensional nature by helping you acknowledge and release the blockages that have been preventing you from knowing your unlimited, multidimensional self.

It is important to know that you are not your body and you are not the brain attached to your body. You are not your ego. If you believe that your body is YOU, then you will not know your infinite self. Your body is only a vehicle that allows you to experience physical reality, but it is not the whole of who you are. Your body operates much like a car, and you are the driver of your car. As a multidimensional being, you exist beyond the third dimensional constructs of linear space and time.

When you meditate, pray, imagine, focus your intentions, and have visionary experiences that move through your heart, you can access multidimensional aspects of yourself, which are likened to stepping outside of a car. This is where you will discover that a larger world exists all around you. If you always remain inside your car, you will only see the world through a windshield. You can experience a deeper, more meaningful life by simply changing your focus and tapping into other levels of consciousness.

This chapter will explain how your consciousness is woven throughout the fabric of the universe, because every vibration that exists in the body of creation is always linked to you. When you ask to know more, you will. When you want to see more, you will. When you know that your beliefs, attitudes and choices directly shape your life, you will begin to see yourself as a co-creator and an alchemist, who can shape whatever you want into physical reality. When you come to know your multidimensional nature, you will be set free from all limitations and you will be able to experience a world that is much greater and richer than you once thought.

Transcribed From:
The Voice of Creation

. . . .

"The key to growth is the introduction of higher dimensions of consciousness into our awareness."
– *Lao Tzu, author of "Tao Te Ching" and the founder of philosophical Taoism*

René Descarte, the French philosopher and mathematician is known for proving that consciousness exists because we can think and we have thoughts. He postulated that it is impossible to doubt that you are thinking, because the mere act of doubting involves thinking; hence his famous quote was born: "I think; therefore I am." It is a simple concept, but it clearly reminds us that there is something more going on beyond just brainwaves and cognition. You are a spiritual being capable of observation, perception, and self-expression.

The ability to observe and be self-aware is the result of consciousness. Your consciousness is also multidimensional, because it is not confined to existing only in a third dimensional framework. You also have the ability to visualize, imagine, plan ahead, and dream of the reality that you want to experience. The ability to shift into other states of consciousness, use your imagination, and bring ideas into fruition, are timeless achievements of consciousness, which occur, because your consciousness is multidimensional.

The Multidimensional Nature Of Consciousness

To better understand the multidimensional nature of consciousness, we must first understand what it is not. Consciousness does not exist within the physical brain and it is not constructed from what you postulate with your 5 senses. It may seem logical that your ability to be aware is because your 5 senses are in full operation, bringing you the ability to see, hear, smell, taste, and touch. However, if you existed in isolation and all of your 5 senses were removed, you would still exist as a sentient being. Your consciousness is able to experience life *through* your senses, but *you* are not your senses. You are also not your brain nor are you just a body. You drive your brain and you drive your body. Your consciousness is the driving force that operates, observes, and experiences life through various gateways. It is the "you" behind the wheel.

Some neuroscientists and biologists continue to scan the brain looking for solid proof that the thinker behind the thought must exist somewhere in the brain. However, as more parts of the brain are studied and analyzed, scientists are concluding that a central region for consciousness simply does not exist. Questions of consciousness have perplexed scientists for years. How can we experience various wavelengths of light and perceive these as colors instead of just bits of data? Why does a composite of musical notes become music to our ears and not just a series of notes? How can dreams and imagination be experienced in the absence of physical stimuli?

When you dream, you are able to experience sound, sight, touch, taste, smell, thought, and emotion. It would seem that your physical body's sensory system would need to be stimulated in order to perceive such sensations. Yet, when you dream, you are able to experience sentient awareness without the need for any outside stimuli. Additionally, your physical body reacts to the *perceived* stimuli, which affects your blood pressure, breathing patterns, and heart rate. How is this possible without the external stimuli to engage your senses?

In the dream example, it is evident that consciousness exists without the need for physical stimuli. We also know that consciousness exists *beyond* wakefulness or sleep, because consciousness has been proven to exist even when there has been a total loss of brain function from either a traumatic brain injury, or death, as mentioned in Chapter One.

With all of this taken into consideration, we can begin to see that human consciousness is actually multidimensional, existing beyond our third dimensional space-time reality. Consciousness exists in the absence of physical stimuli, in the absence of the brain's ability to function, and it continues to exist even when the physical body completely fails us – in the event of death.

What Our Five Senses Do Not Tell Us

We have been taught that our five senses define what is real, but in actuality, our senses only transmit information to our brain, which interprets data, so our consciousness can *observe* the experience. When you look at a red rose, your eyes receive the visual stimuli when light strikes either the rods or cones of the retina. This light converts into electro-chemical signals, which are delivered to the back of the brain, where no light exists.

What are actually just waves, existing as a frequency of energy within the visible spectrum of light, become electrochemical signals produced by the brain. In order for this interaction to become anything more than particles of light and brain waves, there must be a perceiver to interpret the experience. Who is this perceiver that you call 'you' who is seeing and interpreting what you identify as a beautiful red rose?

A similar situation occurs when you *smell* a rose. Microscopic molecules are released from the rose that find their way to hair-like projections in your nose called cilia, which become signals that your brain registers as a "scent". All that is occurring is a reaction between molecules and receptors, and yet, you are able to have the experience of smelling a beautiful rose.

Consciousness is the fabric of your soul and it is the 'you' behind the wheel. This is the 'you' that is not your ego self, but this is the self that is aware of itself before identifying itself with any labels. It is the 'you' that simply is, without applying any conditions or taking on any attachments. It is the 'you' that is the observer, which always has the free will to decide *how* you will observe or perceive anything. This is your authentic self.

Your Multidimensional Self In A Multidimensional Universe

We live in a multidimensional universe that consists of probabilities and potential outcomes, and the probable outcomes in all of your experiences are based on three factors:

1. Your thoughts and perceptions about any situation
2. Your emotional reaction to your experiences
3. Your heartfelt intentions.

The combined energetic output of your thoughts, perceptions and emotions, creates the vibration of your consciousness. The vibration of your consciousness can change at any time, because you always have a choice about how you will perceive and react to anything.

Your ability to perceive can be likened to weighing something on a scale. Depending on how you perceive any situation, your perception can tip the scale more towards the positive side or it can tip the scale more towards the negative side. You get to decide where you will tip your scale. When you believe that something is more possible than impossible and when you choose to have an optimistic outlook, then your scale will tip and lean further towards the positive side.

Suppose you lose your job after working for a company for 25 years. Times like these can be difficult, because it is easy to feel blind-sided when faced with the unexpected. Remember, that you still have a choice about how you can perceive any situation, even during life's most challenging moments.

You can choose to feel devastated like the world has come to an end and you might tell yourself that you will never find another job as good as the last one. Alternatively, you can tell yourself that there is a greater reason why you lost your job and although you don't know the reasons yet, you can choose to believe that something better is going to come out of the experience.

When you believe there is a better job that awaits you, or that there will be new paths leading you to new opportunities, you will start to notice that your environment will match your perceptions. Likewise, if you hold onto the belief that you will never find a job as good as the last one, you will miss any golden opportunities that present themselves, so long as you cling to what's going wrong instead of what's going right.

The next time you are faced with a challenging situation, ask yourself, "Where does my perception fall on the positive/negative scale? How can I change my perception to be more positive to reflect the most positive outcome I can imagine?" There are an infinite number of ways you can perceive any situation just as there are an infinite number of solutions and probable outcomes.

The universe is going to give you what you believe to be true, regardless of which direction your scale is tipping. This is why it is important to become aware of *how* you perceive and define your circumstances. No one wants to have negative experiences or intentions; however, people have negative intentions all the time without realizing it. Negative intentions occur when you *believe* that negative things are going to happen or are happening. What you believe is what you intend, so it is important to change your beliefs to be positively aligned with what you *want* to happen. If you want a positive outcome, then it is important to believe you can experience a positive outcome no matter what situation you find yourself in.

We often forget that we are energetic, spiritual beings, and not limited to having just a physical existence. Our consciousness is fluid and we are all connected to a larger universe. Our thoughts and intentions are extremely powerful, because they can impact and influence our physical reality – whether we are conscious of this or not.

As an energetic being, your vibrational frequency is constantly sending signals out into the universe. This happens because your thoughts and emotions exert a detectable magnetic field. Whether your thoughts are positive, or negative, you are constantly radiating waves of energetic currents. On the universal grid of consciousness, your energy combines with similar energetic vibrations that already exist on the grid.

The universal grid can be compared to a Genesis Pattern. (Fig 11) Imagine this geometric shape as the gridwork, which upon energy flows through the universe. The intersection points are the precise locations where your energetic vibration intersects with another vibration of the same frequency. Your consciousness is constantly shifting and realigning itself to a new location on the grid that is most reflective of your current vibration.

Image of a Genesis Pattern

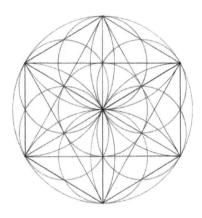

(Figure – 11)

As your expel emotional energy out into the universe, your energy crisscross with other bands of energy in a mathematically orchestrated arrangement, which leads to the manifestation of a reality that is most in alignment with your core beliefs, perceptions, and emotions. All the surrounding space in between the lines gives the *illusion* of form and shape, which we call matter.

Since geometric shapes cannot emerge without precise intersecting lines, then we can see how energy is the basic requirement for creating matter. Our third dimensional experience manifests because we, as beings of consciousness, observe patterns created from intersecting bands of energy. We observe and interpret patterns, shapes, and objects into our everyday experiences from what are fundamentally just intersecting waves of energetic lines.

Everything you perceive in physical reality is comprised of neutral waves of energy, with no inherent meaning. How you choose to perceive your experience is how you will define it. For example, when you feel good about yourself, self-empowered, and at ease, you will start to see and experience a world that supports this reality. Likewise, if you feel worthless, powerless, and drift from one dramatic moment to the next, you will see and experience a world that supports this reality, where you are a helpless victim being swallowed up in a world of chaos.

What you perceive, intend, and believe to be true, is what you will create, because you are constantly "shaping" your world through your perceptions. We are all *shaping* our own lives through our perceptions and interpretations.

Every time you shift your awareness, perceptions, and emotions, your vibrational energy will shift and align itself to a new location on the grid. Since consciousness exceeds space and time and is not limited to the third dimension, then your consciousness can be focused anywhere on the grid. Whatever you can imagine to be true indicates that the energetic wave or probability already exists, and by believing in it, you will match your vibration to it.

Parallel Universes

In 1954, Hugh Everett III, a young Princeton University Doctoral candidate acknowledged that there are parallel universes that are related to our own universe.[46] These universes consist of an infinite number of probable outcomes that can materialize at any point in our physical world. From our third dimensional perspective, we can only focus our consciousness on one locality. We cannot perceive all of these parallel universes at the same time, even though they exist simultaneously.

According to Everett, quantum objects split apart in the universe and can behave as either a particle or a wave.[46] The universe is duplicating itself constantly and creating a new possible outcome in every instance and the parallel reality that you experience is going to be based on how you perceive and react to the "now". There are an infinite number of possibilities that can occur in a single moment.

Anything you can imagine already exists somewhere in a parallel universe; otherwise you would not be able to imagine it. There is nothing that exists outside of creation. Therefore, whatever you think and imagine as a possibility must exist in another reality somewhere. If you can imagine yourself winning the lottery, then there is a parallel universe where this is occurring. If you can imagine living on the earth where all of its inhabitants are nonviolent and unconditionally loving, then this reality exists within a parallel universe. If you can imagine that all elephants are pink, then this too is a reality in another parallel universe. The very fact that you can imagine it means that it exists as a parallel universe.

Parallel universes that exist in close proximity to the current vibrational state of your consciousness will materialize more readily than those that are further away from your current vibration. For example, when you make changes in your perceptions and emotions with the intention of reaching personal goals such as losing weight, obtaining a new job, or attracting more wealth and abundance into your life, it is easier to materialize these types of experiences if you believe that these things are possible, as opposed to trying to manifest something that is far removed from what you think is possible. Your personal vibration must match the vibratory frequency within a parallel universe, before you can experience it.

Your Multidimensional Consciousness And Parallel Realities

You are automatically shifting into parallel realities all the time. We can better understand how we exist in a multiverse when we think of the universe consisting of a series of infinite still frames, which we can call probabilities. Each still frame is slightly varied, as you move from one frame to the next; similar to the way a projector reads a filmstrip.

Your consciousness is sorting through a series of still frames or probabilities, billions of times per second, which gives you the illusion that you are moving through time. However, what is actually happening is your consciousness is shifting in and out of these still frames, as your vibration realigns itself on the universal grid. These alignments create a series of timelines or probable timelines, which we will discuss more in Chapter 5.

As you shift from one parallel reality to another, you are re-creating the past, present, and future versions of yourself in every instant. The memory of your past is only a perception about *what you think* happened. Memories are always based on *perceived* ideas about the past, because the only time that exists is within the present.

The past cannot be re-experienced again other than through a memory. Therefore, the past exists in the same way that any future probability exists: As energetic intersection points on the universal grid. This means that you can choose to align with the same past you have always had or you can choose to align with a different past, simply by shifting your perception about the past.

When you redefine your past, by changing your perceptions and responses to it, you will affect your future timelines too, because you are changing the vibration of your consciousness. You will shift to the reality that best reflects your total vibration, based on the sum of your beliefs, emotional responses, and thoughts about how you relate to your past, present, and future. Physical reality is malleable and pliable, because it is always linked to whatever state of consciousness you are in, within the vibration of "now".

If you can imagine it, think about it, and focus on it, then there is a parallel reality where it exists, regardless of whether we call something *the past*, *the present*, or *the future*. With this expanded awareness, you can decide what kind of past you want to claim from your present point of view, just as you can focus your intention on the kind of future you desire. Your present point of view is always where you have the power to express your consciousness, and you can choose to shift to the most positive vibration of "now" that you can possibly imagine for yourself.

Your perception of the past only stays the same because you are choosing to have the same experience of the past in every parallel universe you are shifting into. However, once you begin to see yourself as a multidimensional being that is recreating yourself in every instance, you can learn to manipulate your own past, present, and future timelines, so you can have more conscious control over the parallel realities you wish to experience in each moment of "now".

Déjà Vu

Déjà Vu is when your consciousness becomes aware of and experiences more than one parallel reality at the same time. I had a memorable Déjà Vu experience one afternoon while my husband and I were driving to a bed and breakfast for a mini vacation. We got lost in the middle of Oregon's wine country, as we drove through the alternating landscapes of tireless lush forests and open fields.

Our car's GPS did not recognize the road we needed to turn onto, so we drove past our destination without realizing it. We continued to travel up the road for about another mile in search of the address but to no avail. Just as we were about to turn around at the entrance of an unnamed gravel road, I noticed there was something very familiar about that road.

In that moment, I slipped into a Déjà Vu awareness and started to recognize everything around me – the gravel road, the rolling hills and trees, all appeared like images from a well-read children's storybook.

I said to my husband, "This road is so familiar and since I am having Déjà Vu right now, I think this road is going to lead us to our bed and breakfast destination. Don't worry about the GPS. I want to follow my gut and see where this road takes us."

As we drove up this familiar road that should have been *unfamiliar*, I realized the timing for this to happen could not have been more perfect. My husband and I were provided with the extra guidance we needed, because that road led us directly to our bed and breakfast destination. The parallel reality awareness I gained from having Déjà Vu served as my internal GPS system.

Imagination And The Time Space Barrier

In addition to being able to tap into parallel realities and multiple timelines with our consciousness, we also have the ability to experience our multidimensional nature through our imagination. Every invention began as a thought. You are the inventor and the creator of your life, because you have the ability to imagine a potential outcome or a probability.

What do you want to experience or change in your life right now? Your imagination has the power to draw up its own mentally constructed blueprints, which are the first steps for transforming thoughts into physical reality.

The more detailed you imagine your desired outcome to be, as you clarify your dreams, the sooner you will begin to notice opportunities streaming into your life. You can imagine *how* you are going to accumulate wealth, *how* you will lose unwanted weight, and *how* you will take the steps to manifest a different line of work. You control the depth of your thoughts, and although the outcome may not be exactly as you imagine, the act of using your imagination and intending a desired change is the recipe behind every great invention.

The word "imagination" means that "I" am the "magician" of my "nation". What you conceive in your mind has the power to transform an entire nation. That is just how powerful you are and why you need to remember this fourth "I AM" Principle, so you will know how your consciousness exists multidimensionally, beyond space and time.

You are creating and re-creating a new version of yourself in every moment, and the creation of self always takes place in every moment of "now" – all within your imagination. You are constantly making choices from one moment to the next, about how you will perceive your past, how you will envision your future, and how you will perceive your present experience. The creation of yourself and your reality always happen within the present moment. This is true whether you are visiting memory lane, thinking about your future, or focused only on the present. You are only able to experience reality from the perspective of "now" no matter what you choose to think about. They key is to make every moment of "now" exactly the way you want it.

The reason we experience the same outcome is because we imagine the same ideas and beliefs again and again. If you are someone who worries a lot about the future or thinks there won't ever be enough money, then this is what you will experience and continue to experience in your parallel realities. However, if you change your perceptions, beliefs, and desires, about what you believe is possible and true; your physical experiences will change. You will literally shift to a parallel universe where these alternate outcomes already exist.

When you imagine the reality you want right now, you are selecting the blueprint that is required prior to receiving it. Don't let worry and fear drive you to imagine a dreadful future that you don't want. Instead of allowing the fear-based ego to steer your imagination, and take you to parallel realities where there is limitation and lack, you can choose to imagine a reality that is filled with infinite possibilities, abundance, and solutions to every problem. Both types of parallel universes exist. Why not choose the universe you prefer instead of the one you fear? You can choose the type of future you want by imagining it positively and wholeheartedly, and by believing and trusting that you can have whatever you want. The only one stopping you – is you.

When You Change Yourself, You Change The World

As you take the initiative to direct your beliefs, perception, and responses, you will notice that those around you will change along with you. It is not that other people are actually changing. What is happening is that you are perceiving and experiencing a different parallel universe where different versions of these same people exist. As you become more peaceful within yourself, you will start to notice a world that reflects peace back to you. When you feel loving, you will notice love everywhere. Likewise, when you feel like nothing is going your way, this will also be reflected back to you. The universe operates just like a hologram. When you change one aspect of the hologram, you affect the entire universe.

The nature of a hologram is that the macro and the micro are always connected. It is impossible for you to make a choice or complete a task that will not affect anyone or anything else around you. You are the ripple in the pond. You are a vibrational wave that spans out across the entire universe of creation. What you think and what you do has a much larger impact on the collective than you are aware of. If you want to change the world, you will do so, simply by making a change within yourself.

When you follow your highest excitement and only do those things that bring you the greatest joy, you will be aligning with your higher self. Your higher self is simply a higher vibrational version of you, which already exists in the multiverse. You will find that there is always a higher version of your higher self, because you are a multidimensional being, constantly expanding and replicating.

Creation is infinite and you can connect to the highest version of yourself whenever you want, simply by entertaining the most positive thoughts and emotions you can imagine. When you allow yourself to remain in an elated state of joy and bliss, and take this as high as you can, for as long as you can, you will leap to a parallel reality that is higher in vibration than you existed in previously. When you follow your passion and share your true self with others, you will find an entire world of other people, whose vibration will be a match to yours.

There Are Many States Of Consciousness

We all experience many states of consciousness everyday. There are times when you are focused in the present, which is when you are living in the now. If you practice yoga, meditation, or deep breathing exercises, this can help bring your focus to the present moment. You will also be focused on the present while you are busy concentrating on a task at work, or while you are engaged in a hobby, music, or art – but present-focused thought is rarely where the mind will stay.

The mind is meant to wander, because this is the normal expression of our multidimensional nature. The problem is that when the mind wanders, the negative ego often becomes the one in charge. When this happens, enthusiasm and joy can quickly transform into fear and worry.

For example, you may be blissfully inspired through a fantasy or dream to start a new business or do something you feel passionate about. Feelings of elation and excitement come from your higher self or higher mind. However, your dream can come to a screeching halt if you listen to the critical mind. The negative ego is skilled at squashing dreams and telling you all the ways that something won't work. A wandering mind is only dangerous when it's driven by the ego.

Whenever we have negative thoughts or feelings, this is our cue to become more aware of how the negative ego is influencing us. It does not have to be this way. We always have a choice. Are you going to listen to your negative ego that criticizes and convinces you that your dreams cannot come true, or are you going to focus on positive thoughts, that will fill your heart with passion and joy? When we welcome and allow imaginative thoughts to enter our mind, and we don't try to stop this flow by siding with the negative ego, we will be led to live the life we truly desire.

Each one of us actually has two minds characterized by two halves of the brain called the left brain and right brain. Your right brain connects to the link, which is the portal where new insights come through, where you will discover infinite creative solutions to every problem, where expansive possibilities are the norm, and where you will find your genius. Your left brain is where your critical ego resides, which is characterized by linear, rule-oriented thinking.

Brain scientist, and public speaker, Jill Bolte Taylor, had a stroke that damaged the left-hemisphere of her brain at the age of 37. During the midst of her stroke, she observed her own brain's functionalities shut down one by one – as her motion, speech, memory, and self-awareness faded away. All she was left with was the ability to think only with the right hemisphere of her brain. While Taylor spent the next eight years recovering her ability to think critically, walk, and talk, she will never forget the euphoric experience of losing the functionality of the left side of her brain.[47]

Her perceived sense of individuality and seeing herself as separate from the world vanished. She instantly saw herself as pure energy and felt one with everything around her. She observed this not only through a mental and spiritual shift in her awareness, but also through her physical sense of self as well. When she looked down at her arms and legs, all she saw were the atoms in her body blending with the atoms in the space that surrounded her. Today, she shares her experience through public presentations and through her book entitled, "My Stroke of Insight, A Brain Scientist's Personal Journey", which has provided a scientific breakthrough in brain research.[47]

We use the left and right hemispheres of our brain interchangeably. The left hemisphere compartmentalizes, separates, and labels everything; whereas the right hemisphere notices patterns and connectivity to everything. They have opposite functions, and at times, you may notice that your right and left hemispheres are in conflict with one another.

For example, you may find yourself in the midst of a pleasant fantasy, feeling very excited about something you've always wanted to do or experience, but then the critical left side of the brain chimes in and says, "You will never make any money doing that!" Or, "People will think you're crazy!" Or, "You don't have time to chase your silly dreams. You have to go to work and raise a family." Or, "That's not a good idea. It's probably already been created, invented, or thought of." We have all heard this negative chatter and it's very destructive, because it stops us from doing what we truly love.

When your ego or left brain is dominant, your dreams will deflate, because the negative ego will always focus on limitation and impossibilities. The higher mind is linked to your creative, right brain, which is where your imagination comes through, guiding you towards infinite possibilities.

If you were to pursue your dreams and follow only the imaginative thoughts that bring you the greatest joy and excitement, without allowing your ego to present you with limitations, restrictions, fear, and worry, then you would be following the path towards higher consciousness, which is in harmony with your higher self. You always have the choice to experience life any way you want – either through the ego's limited perspective, or you can experience your multidimensional higher self, which is limitless.

When the negative ego is in charge, we dread the past and fear the future. The ego interferes with everything we feel passionate about by destroying our dreams, yet the only way for creation to emerge, is *through our dreams*. Our dreams are the foundation of the co-creative experience. This is the link to your Godself.

As co-creators in a physical existence, we are meant to experience and explore our full multidimensional selves, as both the dreamer and the dreamed. The idea is not only to dream, but also to dream as big as we can. We will feel intense passion and excitement coming from the heart and it will feel as though we have returned home. This is because when we live out our dreams, we are answering the call from our higher self.

The Co-Existence Of Multiple Dimensions

We live on a physical planet that is comprised of a first, second, third, and fourth dimension, which are interwoven together. A single point in space defines the first dimension. The second dimension is defined by a straight line, which travels from point A to point B. The third dimension is any object that has height, width, and depth, creating mass and solidity, which we define as physical reality. The fourth dimension is a timeless dimension, which is where thought, creativity, and the spiritual (astral plane) are rooted.

The fourth dimension appears to be rooted in space-time, when we perceive this from a linear third dimensional perspective. However, there is no linear time beyond the third dimension. Dreaming, astral travel, and accessing our imagination, are fourth dimensional points of consciousness, which is actually the dimension of *timelessness* and not one of *time*.

Human beings are able to perceive all dimensions within the first, second, third, and fourth dimensional spectrum. This is because this is the collective level of ascension where our consciousness resides at this time. Although higher dimensions exist beyond the four that we experience, and continue to interweave within all of the other dimensions, we are not aware of these other dimensions, simply because our consciousness is not evolved enough to perceive them. However, as we ascend spiritually and become more aware of our multidimensionality, we will begin to perceive and integrate these higher dimensions into our overall experience.

The fourth dimension is fluid, maliable, timeless, and filled with infinite possibilities. It is non-material and non-linear, bypassing the space-time barrier. The third dimension is one step down, which is the material expression of the creative, fourth dimension. Seeing the ways that our thoughts create reality is demonstrative of how the fourth dimension affects the third dimension.

When you are dreaming, meditating, imagining or visualizing something, your consciousness is actually tapping into the fourth dimension, which is the dimension that exists beyond linear time. When you are sleeping and having a dream, your consciousness is more concentrated in the fourth dimension, which is why your dreams and your surroundings can change in a flash and why you are not aware of the passage of time while you are dreaming. The fourth dimension is void of time. When existing in this realm, you are timeless and your experience does not happen in a linear fashion the way you perceive time in the third dimension. When you go from sleeping to wakefulness, you are literally shifting from fourth dimensional awareness to third dimensional awareness.

Your mind, or your consciousness crosses the time-space barrier all the time, several times each day. These are the times when your awareness shifts away from your physical surroundings and you experience daydreams or enter a dreamlike state of consciousness.

You may have had the common experience of driving your car on a long journey, but as you grew bored with driving, imaginative thoughts entered your mind. This is because you shifted from third dimensional awareness to fourth dimensional awareness, which are natural shifts in consciousness. You suddenly find yourself at your destination without any memory of the drive or how you got there. The passage of time is different from one dimension to the next, because in the fourth dimension, there is no time. We only perceive time when we are focused in the third dimension.

Everything you plan on doing in the future must be thought of first, no matter how small the task may seem. For example, as you drive home from work you may think, "What am I going to have for dinner once I get home?"

In the moment that you have this thought, visual images appear in your mind. This may be portrayed as images of seeing yourself buying food at the supermarket, or you may see yourself preparing and cooking the food, or you may imagine yourself standing in front of the refrigerator trying to remember what ingredients you have to work with.

In contemplating any of these scenarios you are engaged in *multidimensional mind travel*. This is when your consciousness temporarily leaves the third dimension and moves into timelessness, which is non-physical awareness.

You did not physically complete the task of making dinner as you drove home, but you saw yourself making dinner through your imagination. While your physical body cannot move through time and space in an instant, your mind clearly can, and does this all the time.

Our ability to transcend space and time with our consciousness is often misunderstood. Many think that imagination is nothing more than fantasy or child's play, but the ability to travel into higher dimensions with our consciousness is the most powerful, natural ability we have. The more we become aware that our consciousness is fluid and exists beyond the third dimension of physicality, the more we can tune into our multidimensional nature.

Before Thomas Edison invented the light bulb, he had to first believe in the *possibility* of a light bulb and he had to imagine it with his mind before he could bring it to life. It took him hundreds of attempts before he finally struck light. Once Edison shifted the imagined light bulb into physical existence, the world changed. By believing in his dream, Thomas Edison manifested a product that is used by people everywhere in the world. Everything that has ever been engineered or invented first came into existence through the imagination.

Fourth Dimensional Mind Travel Is What Shapes Your Third Dimensional Reality

Fourth dimensional mind travel is what brings everything into physical existence. Without our ability to visualize what is possible for the future, conceive new ideas and expand on existing ones, we would not be enjoying the technological advances of today.

As our consciousness shifts back and forth between the fourth and third dimensions, what we are actually doing is transforming energy into matter. You have the ability to decide what matters and what doesn't matter with your consciousness. When something "matters", this word literally means that you are making something materialize. When something does not matter to your consciousness, it won't materialize and it will remain in its original energetic state.

You share a planet with many other creatures, but your ability to be self-aware and turn fourth dimensional thought into third dimensional experiences is unique to your human spirit. Humans are the only creatures on Earth that are aware of their relationship with time and space, and can transform imaginative thought into a physical experience.

When you look down at an anthill on a warm summer day, you can observe the ants, but they do not have the conscious capacity to look up and see you observing them. They also can't look up to see the stars and sky above, and they cannot acknowledge that a larger universe exists outside of their domain.

A dog gets up each day. He eats, plays, sleeps, looks after his owner, and lives life as a dog, but a dog is unable to plan his life around time. Your dog does not celebrate birthdays, schedule appointments, nor does he contemplate life and death, because he is unconscious of the fourth dimension of space-time.

Although ants, dogs, and other creatures are not aware that they exist in a fourth dimension, this does not mean that a fourth dimension does not exist along side them. We live in a multidimensional universe where numerous dimensions exist simultaneously within our own plane of existence. Most people cannot experience their consciousness beyond the fourth dimension, but this does not mean that higher dimensions do not exist.

It is likely that a multitude of dimensions and other life-forms exist within what we understand as the first, second, third, and fourth dimensions, but most of us are not able to perceive the beings that dwell in these higher dimensions. The level of our consciousness determines the dimensional existence we will experience.

Consciousness is always evolving and ascending. One day, the collective human consciousness will be ready to progress to the next dimension, which we will refer to as the fifth dimension.

Merging Into The Fifth Dimension

On the night of November 1, 1993, I had a visitation from a being that was not from this planet. This particular being appeared to be angelic or divine in many ways. As I reflect on this encounter, I feel confident that visits from angelic beings reported throughout history, might have actually been visits from this same type of extraterrestrial that visited me. This being was highly evolved – both spiritually and intellectually.

I woke up at approximately 3:30 in the wee hours of the morning, and saw a small female child hovering slightly above the foot of my bed. If I were to guess her age, based on her stature, mannerisms, and the sound of her voice, she appeared to be about 4 or 5 years old.

She was wearing a white gown and her hair was very thin and light blond in color. She had bright blue eyes and a high forehead, or perhaps her forehead looked like it was high because her hair was thin and her cranium was much larger proportionally than her frail, petite body. She had fair, milky-white skin, and her entire body illuminated and radiated some type of white glowing light. This explains how I was able to see her so clearly, even though it was dark in my bedroom.

Her eyes were beautiful and a bit larger than what you would expect to see in a child. She had a narrow chin, and her mouth turned downward, but when she spoke, her mouth did not move. Her communication was telepathic. Not only did I hear her words spoken directly inside my head, but she also sent vivid images into my mind. It was as though movie clips or still pictures were being displayed in my head, as if to illustrate everything she was telling me.

I was awestruck by the distinct child-like innocence in her voice and gestures, similar to the charm of an adorable 4-year-old, yet her intelligence and wisdom surpassed my own adult intelligence.

She said telepathically, "Our fifth dimensional world is going to merge and co-exist with your fourth dimensional world." She held up her hand and showed me five fingers and then four fingers as a child often does when communicating numbers. She continued, "Your earth is going to change when this happens."

Animated images of ghosts or spirits entered my mind, unlike anything I have ever imagined. These ghosts or spirits were loving and kind and they dwelled visibly upon the earth, along-side people, as if to demonstrate how the spiritual realm and the physical realm would no longer be on separate planes. I wasn't frightened by anything she was showing me, because there wasn't anything that struck me as negative. I was also told that any negative entities would not be able to live on the earthly plane once the two dimensions merged, and human beings would become more loving and more unified with one another as a result.

I asked if natural disasters would still exist on the earth after the merging takes place. She said they would still exist. She then showed me images of a father and his son being rocked by an earthquake. The man was holding his son in his arms and neither of them looked frightened by the earthquake. They were calm, trusting, and in harmony with the earth. They even smiled while they experienced the earthquake.

She said, "The work is almost done." She showed me several images of children that looked a bit like her. I knew that all of those children would be merging to live harmoniously with us, on Earth, at some point in time.

For the next two decades, I reflected on that message and wondered when this dimensional merge would happen. It has since become clear that a veil separating the fourth and fifth dimensions is now thinning, which is what I believe will allow for the merge.

Human consciousness has changed dramatically since that visitation in 1993. At that time, people were more likely to argue *against* the existence of UFO's, life on other planets, and the possibility that other dimensions exist along side ours. Today, we have an expanded understanding about quantum mechanics, space science, and technology, all which has led to the transformation in our consciousness.

The Internet has also led to rapid changes in our consciousness. Social networking and the distribution of information has now become a global exchange instead of a local one. We are connecting to people and information; we wouldn't otherwise be connected to.

With greater access to resources, we now have a much wider range of choices available to us, so we can make more refined choices about what we agree with, disagree with, and who or what we choose to associate with. The mainstream media is no longer considered the only news source.

The idea that we are alone in the universe is becoming less plausible. There has been an increase in the number of television shows that feature real ghost stories, extraterrestrial life, and paranormal phenomenon. Today, more people are reporting that they have seen a ghost or experienced something similar, have had or digitally captured a UFO sighting, or seen something they can't explain in the sky, while many others have also had near-death experiences, astral travel projections, past life memories, and the like. The increased awareness and acceptance that unexplained paranormal realities can co-exist with physical reality, is not as far-fetched as it once was. It is as though a veil is being lifted, as more people become aware that a mysterious and exciting new world may be starting to blend into our existing one.

The fact that you are reading this book is indicative that the merging of dimensions has already begun. When you ascend to higher levels of conscious awareness, the old paradigm of limiting thoughts and beliefs will no longer fit with the changes that are taking place. You will desire a different set of tools to deal with new circumstances.

As more people become aware of their existence beyond the third dimensional grid, and realize that we can manipulate time and space with our mind, there will be a global shift in consciousness. Higher dimensional beings are waiting, ready to welcome us and guide us into our next level in ascension.

We all have the ability to engage in multidimensional mind travel, but most of us have been doing this unconsciously. When the ego-mind is the driver and dictator of our future, our thoughts will appear negative and filled with worry. We can instead, allow positive thoughts to come through our imagination, which will connect us to our higher mind, leading us towards the destination we truly desire.

Each of us has the ability to imagine and create anything we want, but we have been disillusioned and led to believe that there are limitations in our abilities and consciousness. When we worry about the future or when we think we cannot achieve something, we are allowing negativity to seep into our multidimensional mind traveling experience. Most everything we have ever manifested for ourselves has been done unconsciously. If we choose to focus on a future that is filled with worry, failure, uncertainty, or a future that is based in fear, then that is the type of existence we will continue to manifest. When we realize we are multidimensional mind travelers, then every futuristic thought is a reality that already exists in a parallel universe. Once we know this, we can decide which reality we want to become part of.

Indigo Children

The complete merging into fifth dimensional consciousness means that we will no longer be controlled by limited beliefs. To help humanity make this next leap towards ascension, spiritually advanced souls have chosen to incarnate on planet Earth during this critical time. Many refer to these children as Indigo Children. Other names like Crystal Children, Rainbow Children, or Blue Rays have been given to spiritually advanced souls born in the succeeding generations, but Indigo Children are described to be the first wave of souls that arrived to help humanity rise to this next level of fifth dimensional consciousness.

The name "Indigo Child" was first introduced in the 1970's by parapsychologist, Nancy Ann Tappe. The "Indigo Child" describes this special group of children, who not only have unique psychic and paranormal abilities, but their auras are described as having more of an indigo hue compared to other children's auras born during that same time.[48]

Indigo Children are deeply connected to the spiritual side of life and are able to tap into a larger cosmic mind more easily. These children have been described as being very empathetic, sensitive, and it's as though they are 'old souls', coming here to teach, inspire, and help with the spiritual ascension of humanity.

There are many children born today who are labeled as having *learning or behavioral disabilities*, some of whom are diagnosed as having Autism or ADHD (Attention Deficit and Hyperactivity Disorder). Even though we are seeing more children receiving these diagnostic labels, it is not clear whether there is truly an increase in such conditions, or if the increase is because there has been an increase in diagnostic labeling itself.

Receiving a label that you or your child has ADHD or Autism has a much more negative connotation than acknowledging that you or your child is an "Indigo Child". One sends a negative message that there is something wrong and that the individual's cognitive abilities need to be managed differently, whereas being known as an "Indigo Child" sends a positive message that the individual has special talents and this is a welcome change for our world.

Because we live in a society that operates more from the left hemisphere of the brain, society relies on a scientific methodology to define what is "smart" and what is "normal". Any person who thinks or behaves outside of what is considered "mainstream", is perceived as being disruptive to the system. Those that are born with heightened sensitivities to certain things, those that see the world from a different perspective, or those who are passionate, highly energetic, or talented in a specific area, are often discouraged instead of encouraged.

Many "Indigo Children", or those born after this first wave of

"Indigos", are suppressed, medicated, and placed in special education, because they are viewed as having a problem that needs fixing. In reality, these children are *the solution* to problems that have weakened our society. The gifts they've come to share with the world are discredited, simply because these children's abilities are misunderstood.

What likely occurred since the 1970's, is the name "Indigo Child" adopted a different set of labels, which focuses on what the child lacks rather than what the child's strengths are. Educators, parents, and psychologists are quick to label children as having a disability based on poor academic performance, perceived social isolation, motivational weaknesses, among other factors, because the child is not fitting in as "mainstream".

In order for a child to succeed in mainstream education, the child must be pliable, amiable, and follow directions easily. Asking questions or thinking differently, feeling bored and unchallenged, or depressed with the status quo indicates there is a problem, but the problem is not within the child. If we listen to these children, we will see that they are shining their light in a broken world. *The establishments in our world* need fixing, not the child.

There can never be a problem with any individual or what an individual has to offer. Creation does not make mistakes. Everyone holds a piece of the puzzle and we all serve a purpose. Once enough people recognize that thinking outside the box is necessary for progressive transformation, there will be a tipping of the scale. The shift will be so significant; we will wonder why it took so long to realize we had the creative ingenuity to create the changes we desired, all along.

CHAPTER FIVE

YOU ARE TIMELESS, INFINITE, AND ETERNAL

Dear One,

Your need to track time has distracted you and taken you away from your true infinite nature. Why are you in such a hurry? Where are you going? What are you doing? Why are you always chasing a false perception of time, which keeps getting away from you, when real time does not even exist? The illusion of time is a trap, which captures your focus, and where you place your focus is where your consciousness will always follow. Do you really want to focus your consciousness and all of your attention on trying to catch something that is not real? The only real time is "now time", and when you are in this space, this is where you will find the real part of you that is infinite. Chasing time is only going to pull you away from the "now", causing you to forget your true infinite nature.

The joy of living is to live in the joy. Be in the moment as if there is no time. When you watch a duck paddling in a pond, see a bird spread its wings in flight, or observe the beauty in a flower's bloom, realize that real beauty is in the absence of time. The pause is what turns noise into music. Stillness is where you will find the realness of life. There is nothing to chase and there is nothing pushing against the beauty in All That Is. It simply is.

You don't have to work so hard, Dear One. You can take a breath without counting how long it takes before you take your next breath, and you will still remember how to breathe. You can walk to and from your destination without worrying about obstacles or barriers that you think will block you from your future. It is in the journey and not the destination where you will find the greatest lessons and where you will see the greatest beauty. You do not have to run to where you need to go. There is always something that will carry you to wherever you feel you need to run to and you will get there just as you have been destined, if you simply allow the journey to carry you.

Transcribed From:
The Voice of Creation

. . . .

"The only reason for time is so that everything doesn't happen at once."
– *Albert Einstein*

You are timeless, infinite and eternal. You can realign with this zero-point aspect of yourself when you remember what life was like when you were an infant or a small child – always focused on the now, observing each moment as if it were separate and exclusive from any other points in time.

As a baby, you were not aware of any past or future. There was only now. When you observe the moment of now without applying any judgments, labels, or criticism, you will find the "I AM" presence is always at the center of your experience.

Experiencing timelessness is blissfully calming, which is why time seems to pass rapidly when you do something you love or follow that which makes you feel alive, passionate, and excited. There is no other moment like the moment you are experiencing right now. If you could capture this moment and take it with you so it could become a permanent part of you, what is it about this moment that you would want to claim? Can you see the gift, discover the beauty, and see the miracle that lies within the trillions of things that had to come together to make this moment happen? This moment is not like any other moment you have ever experienced before. It never existed in the past and it can never be experienced again in the future, other than as a memory. Each moment of now is an opportunity to extract whatever you can add to your aliveness, joy, and inner truth.

The only way to fully grasp what your moment has in store for you is to be completely absorbed in it. Being present-focused is as easy as setting your intention to do so. There is nothing magical or mysterious about operating from this perspective, because when you were born, this was your innate nature. Therefore, in order to become reconnected with blissful timelessness, all you need to do is shift your focus, and let go of past or future worries, labels, and expectations. You will then become a participant in the authentic moment of "now" and you will become aware that you are the "I" that is the "eye". You are the seer who is capable of observing the present moment just as it is, and when you are in this state, you will gain more energetically from your surroundings.

Experiencing timelessness is about letting go of past beliefs and releasing future expectations so the 'presents' or the gifts in the 'present' can surface. When you tap into your space of timeless awareness, it is normal for thoughts, feelings, and opinions to creep into your mind. You can decide if you want to follow your inner thoughts, feelings, and opinions, or you can simply let them pass by.

When you practice being fully present in the "now", it will be easier to observe thoughts and feelings for what they truly are — just thoughts and feelings. You can *decide* whether you want to give them any attention, react to them, own them, release them, or just observe them.

The more you practice *seeing* from *the observer's* perspective, the easier it will be to recognize that your critiquing ego is not you. You are the observer of everything, including the activity going on in your brain.

You switch your computer on or off, but you are not your computer. Your computer handles the data and processing of information, but you always remain the one who operates your system through your keyboard, monitor, and mouse. Similar to your computer, your brain filters information, labels things, and categorizes information from your observations, but YOU always get to choose how you will respond, because you operate your computer. Your computer does not operate itself.

Your brain continues to formulate new thoughts from old thoughts, and a sea of thoughts and emotions can easily sweep you away from your timeless present experience. However, as soon as you notice the critiquing ego for what it truly is, you can separate your authentic self from any programmed responses. You can remain aware of yourself, as the observer and the operator.

Throughout life, we experience a colorful array of emotions, which stem from our perceptions. There are an infinite number of ways we can perceive something, but there are always just two polarities at the root of every thought or emotion: Positive or negative.

A negative thought causes us to feel limited, constrained, or separate. A positive thought causes us to feel capable, expansive, and unified within the world around us.

Feelings and moods always precede our thoughts, because our emotions are a direct response from the thoughts we are having. If you want to change your mood, then this must be changed at the thought-level and not by trying to change the mood itself.

We all have moments when we are filled with joy and connection and other times when we feel lonely or in despair. We have all experienced anger, jealousy, sadness, or fear during certain moments in our lives, and other times we experience compassion, love, happiness, and confidence.

In spite of the polarity we experience from our thoughts and emotions, the same observer is always there. The "eye" that is the "I" is the one who is always seeing, always observing, always perceiving, and always feeling. You experience your thoughts and emotions but *you are not* those thoughts and emotions. Your thoughts and experiences will always come, go, and change — just like seasons or weather patterns, but you will remain.

Not only do your thoughts come and go, but the cells in your body are also being replaced constantly, so most of the cells you were born with are not the same cells that make up your body today. Biologically, you are not the same person that you were in infancy and yet, you are still the "I" or the observer that continues to have the experience called your life. Even though your body ages and changes its shape and form, you, the observer, do not change.

Your thoughts, beliefs and the types of choices you make are also likely to change throughout the years as you grow and learn new things. Many people change their career path or their life partners several times in one lifetime, because individual thoughts, beliefs, values and ideas of "self" are constantly changing. However the real self, which is the "I" that is the "eye" never changes. This is the only constant that remains unchanged, because the real "I AM" is timeless, infinite and eternal.

When you live in the moment, appreciating all that the "now" has to offer, you will experience timelessness. Your timeless presence is the only thing that is truly eternal. Everything else is temporary.

When you transition and leave this physical dimension, you will not take your physical body with you, nor will you take any of your possessions, occupations, or any ego-based constructs of self. Only the "I AM" consciousness will exit the body. This is also referred to as your soul, which is your energetic essence, capable of observation.

After you have lived your life on Earth, others will not remember you by your labels, such as your occupational title, your successes or failures, nor will you be remembered by your possessions. You will be remembered by the way your presence affected the lives of those around you. You will be remembered for things that are energetic, such as the hugs you gave, the way your smile and laughter filled the room, and the kind-hearted ways you helped others. You will also be known for what your 'being alive' taught others. It is the *essence* of your soul that you leave behind and that you take with you at the same time.

Your soul is not bound by the same limitations as the physical body. The soul's energy can exist in multiple places at the same time. This is very confusing for most people, because human consciousness appears to have only one specific point of focus at a time. We cannot focus on simultaneous existences or be in multiple places at the same time, so how can our soul exist in multiple places at the same time?

The reason is because your soul is energetic and not physical so it can experience multiple incarnations, be in multiple places at the same time, and have multiple experiences simultaneously. The perceived passage of time occurs only while residing in the third dimension. When perceived outside the third dimensional awareness – the past, present, and future probabilities are all happening at the same time.

Our Relative Relationship With Time

When Albert Einstein introduced his Special Relativity theory about time in the early 20th century, he suggested that time wasn't separate from space but it was connected to it, creating space-time. The movement, travel, and passage of time is also relative to the individual's position in space. This means that someone moving through space-time will experience it differently at various points. Time will actually appear to move slower near massive objects, because space-time is warped by the weight of nearby objects.

In 1962, scientists placed two atomic clocks at the bottom and top of a water tower. The clock at the bottom, was closer to the center of the Earth, and that clock ran slower than the clock at the top of the water tower. Einstein called this phenomenon time dilation.[49]

The Twin Paradox is another example of time dilation, devised in 1911 by French physicist Paul Langevin. If one twin lives at the bottom of a mountain and the other lives at the top, the twin closer to the Earth (at the bottom) will age more slowly. He or she would appear younger than the other twin, though by a very small degree. However, if you send one twin in a spaceship accelerating close to the speed of light, he or she would return much younger than the other twin, because the high acceleration and large gravitational masses influence time. Of course, no one has gone as far as to send somebody's twin into high-speed orbit, but scientists proved the hypothesis was true in the 1970s by sending an atomic clock into orbit. When the automic clock returned to the earth, it had run much slower than the atomic clock that had remained on the earth.[49]

What we learned from these experiments is that time is relative and the effect it has on us can vary. Time is not fixed, because when we change our position in space, the speed at which we travel, or our *perception* of time, we find that the passage of time also changes.

Our perception of time is a direct reflection of how we view ourselves. When we punch a time clock or impatiently stare at the clock at work, rush to our next appointment, or scurry to get as many things done in a day as possible, we have forgotten about our own timeless and eternal nature.

When we define the state of our existence as linear and finite, then we perceive the passage of time in this same way. We believe that time is running out and slipping away from us. We must keep up with time, or time will take us down. We try to slow down the aging process, work as hard and as fast as we can, and measure the quality of our life by how busy and productive we are. Rather than embracing the now, which is how we will connect to our timeless nature, we are encouraged to live according to an artificial construct of time.

We believe that our survival depends on committing to a job and maintaining a work schedule. We believe that we will not make enough money to care for our basic survival needs if we believe in a timeless existence. However, operating from the perspective that time is linear is merely an illusion that has been perpetuated by westernized society. It has been serving the corporations very well, but this is not our true nature.

We have been encouraged to maintain a constant schedule, pay attention to the clock, and that our successes or failures are measured by how quickly we get from point A to point B. We believe in phrases like, "time is money," "don't waste time," and "don't be lazy." This conditioning has led us to fear our own timelessness, which is to simply exist as fully as we can in the moment of now. There is no other time other than this.

Once we become aware that living within linear time is merely a concept constructed out of westernized conditioning, we can realize that we have a choice. We can choose to stay connected to the artificial construct of linear time, or we can choose to operate more from a *here and now* perspective – which is void of fear, expectations, judgment, and criticism.

When we hold onto the belief that *time is money* or that our survival depends on *punching a time clock everyday*, then we hold onto beliefs that reinforce limitations. As long as we believe that time is linear, or that time will run out, we lose our connection to our timeless nature, which is infinite, creative, and expansive.

Whenever we lose ourselves in a daydream, connect to nature and the outdoors, or lose track of time by doing something we love, shame and guilt often follows. This is because we have been conditioned to believe that something must be wrong with us if we step too far away from our linear focus.

In reality, there is nothing wrong with us when we step into our timeless nature. When we let go of the need to be at a certain place at a certain time, we can live more fully as a timeless being and remember our infinite nature. We can learn to embrace any interruptions along the way and stop worrying whether everything will go as planned. We were born with the infinite stillness of the "I AM" presence, and this stillness is always within each one of us. We will instantly regain our awareness of this presence whenever we step out of the time trap – and just BE in the now.

Living within the limitations of linear time does not allow much space to be the director of our own life and live according to the way we want to live. Instead, we are living life by a set of obligations and perceived expectations. When we express our sense of timelessness, we will live fearlessly. We will be motivated by our inner passion and excitement, rather than living according to what the outside world expects from us.

When you take control of your timeless nature, you are taking control of your destiny. You are free to do all those things you love to do instead of doing things you "think" you "should" do. When you live this way, you are shifting from third dimensional consciousness to fourth dimensional consciousness and this can happen in an instant. The awareness that you are timeless and multidimensional is the true nature of who you are.

The Perception Of Time According To Our Ancient Ancestors

Before we *go back in time* and peek into our ancestor's past, it is important to fully understand that the westernized ideology surrounding linear time parallels the state of our collective consciousness. Just like linear time, our own existence appears to consist of only a beginning, middle, and an end, from a third dimensional view.

When we live within the frames of linear time, we have simultaneously defined our existence as something that is confined by limitation. The idea that you are finite and that once you die, you will no longer exist, simply aligns with the same illusion that parallels the artificial matrix of linear time.

When we hold onto the belief that time is linear and finite, we begin to see ourselves as finite beings, and this prevents us from being able to experience our expansive consciousness that exists beyond our third dimensional awareness. We are more than just third dimensional beings. We are multidimensional beings, having a partial and temporary experience in the third dimension. It is only from the westernized third dimensional perspective, that we began perceiving time in a finite way.

However, this is not the way our ancient ancestors understood time. Our ancestors understood time from a fourth dimensional perspective. To our ancestors, time was not something that was limited, linear, or finite. Instead, time was perceived as cyclical.

We can all agree that it takes approximately 24 hours for the earth to complete a rotation on its axis. Our planet makes one revolution around the sun every 365.25 days, and the earth's axis completes one full cycle of precession approximately every 26,000 years. We observe the passage of time when we watch a sunrise and a sunset, experience the changing seasons, enjoy another birthday celebration, or look through photo albums from our past.

The difference is that from a third dimensional perspective, we experience time as having a beginning, middle, and an end. Our ancestors were able to tap into a greater fourth dimensional awareness of space-time, in which they embraced their infinite nature by embodying the *cycles* of time.

Our ancestors' celebrations and ceremonies recognized astrological shifts as they moved from one age to another, or whenever they entered into a new cycle or loop of time. Our ancestors had a deeper awareness of spiritual realms and enjoyed regular contact with spirit guides or guardians, and this was because their relationship with time was harmonious with fourth dimensional consciousness.

Many ancient philosophies and religions believed in reincarnation. The idea that a soul incarnates again and again coincides with the idea that time is not only cyclical and eternal, but so is our consciousness.

It wasn't until we grew disconnected from nature, at the time of the industrial revolution, that we started to live within a finite understanding of time. The state of our own consciousness and how we began to define ourselves followed along this same path. However, when we step outside of this artificial linear time matrix by living in the moment of now, by communing with nature, or by losing ourselves in something we enjoy doing that we feel passionate about, we can easily shift away from the limitations of third dimensional consciousness. We can shift back into a less restrictive, fourth dimensional awareness, just like our ancestors were connected to.

Tribal societies, hunters and gatherers, and agricultural societies, are tuned into the cycles of nature for survival. The farmer needs to constantly be aware that time is cyclical in order to tend to the crops and be aware of the changing seasons. A successful farmer knows to expect that some months will have more rainfall or be colder than other months. He knows when it's the best time to plant seeds and when it's the best time to harvest, because he is working within the cycles of time and with nature's relationship to time.

When we observe that the passage of time has a relationship to other things and that any event is always an aspect of the whole, we will begin to have a more complete understanding of how time-space truly operates. All we need to do is shift our awareness away from the linear third dimensional perspective to a broader, fourth dimensional awareness.

Every ancient culture, ancient religion, and ancient philosophy, understood that we are infinite beings who are part of a larger universe, webbed in cyclical patterns of time. Buddhists, Jain and Hindu cosmologies all described the universe as having a never-ending series of cycles, each lasting millions or billions of years. All Native American cultures, Mesoamericans, Sumerians, Egyptians, Babylonians, Indians, Chinese, and both the ancient and classical Greeks and Romans also shared this same idea of cyclical time.

"According to Hindu cosmology, life in the universe is created and destroyed once every 4.1 to 8.2 billion years, which is one full (day and night) cycle for Brahma. The lifetime of a Brahma, the Hindu God of creation, may be between 40 billion and 311 trillion years. The cycles are said to repeat like the seasons, waxing and waning within a greater time-cycle of the creation and destruction of our universe. Like Summer, Spring, Winter and Autumn, each yuga involves stages of gradual change, that the earth and the consciousness of mankind goes through as a whole. A complete yuga cycle from a high Golden Age, called the Satya Yuga to a Dark Age, Kali Yuga, and back again, is said to be caused by the solar system's motion around another star." There are a total of four ages that comprise the Yuga Cycle.[50]

The Satya Yuga Age or the Golden Age, is the longest span of time within the Yuga Cycle which lasts 4,800 years. This is a period of time when consciousness is at its peak and the connection to the creator is strongest. People living on earth dwell in total peace and enlightenment during this age. The second age is called the Treta Yuga or the Silver Age which lasts 3,600 years. The Bronze age or the Dwapara Yuga lasts 2,400 years, while the darkest age called Kali Yugi or Iron Age is the shortest age, lasting 1,200 years.[50]

The combined total of the Yuga Cycle is completed in two arcs consisting of 12,000 years each, in which one half of the cycle is ascending in consciousness, and the other half is decending in consciousness, consisting of a total of 24,000 years.

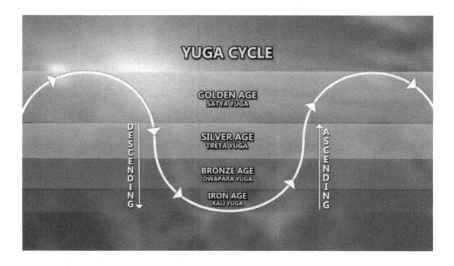

(Figure – 12)

This 24,000 year cycle completes the precession of the equinox. During the ascending half of the cycle, the sun is moving towards the point in orbit that is closest to the galactic center. The descending half of the cycle is when the sun is moving towards the point that is furthest away from the galactic center. (Fig-12)[51]

Like ancient India, the ancient Mayan civilization also understood time to be cyclical. On December 21, 2012, the Mayan Calendar ended with the completion of the Long Count calendar. The December solstice sun became aligned with the center of the Milky Way galaxy at that time, which the ancient Mayan's believe is the Womb of the Great Mother. This occurs only once every 13,000 years and is a similar calculation of time noted by ancient India. This same 13,000 year cycle is responsible for the Golden Age, a period of enlightenment or the end of an old world that succeeds the birth of a new world.[(52)]

Throughout history, civilizations that have never come into contact with one another have a similar understanding that cycles of time have a direct influence on human consciousness. Our ancient ancestors' concept of cyclic time was more widespread and lasted much longer in duration than the westernized concept of linear time. It is as though humanity has regressed in consciousness over the past several hundred years, shifting away from fourth dimensional consciousness to a more restrictive, limited, third dimensional focus.

Could this regression be because over the past 2,400 years we have been descending into the darkest of all of the ages, and could this be the reason why we lost touch with our spiritual nature, thereby affecting our understanding of time? According to the ancients, the state of our consciousness is relative to our planetary position in space. Astrologically, this makes sense. Our level of consciousness may have to do with which side of the Milky Way Galaxy we are in as we cycle through time.

As we descended through the Yuga Cycle and passed through one side of the galaxy, we have been engaged in wars almost constantly, the industrial revolution emerged and created classes of people, and the destruction to the planet became the norm. There definitely appears to be a connection between our planetary cycles and where we are spiritually in our consciousness.

Currently, we are beginning to ascend once again, and we are becoming more spiritual and conscious of other densities and realities. According to our ancient ancestors, we will continue to expand in our consciousness over the next 12,000 years, as we move through this cycle, until we finally reach the Golden Age once again.

After December 21, 2012, our planet passed through the galactic center of the Milky Way as the earth completed its full cycle of the precession of the equinoxes. The Mayan's called this the "universal cycle". The Hopi Native Americans referred to transitional phase as the beginning of the Fifth World. Astrologers have been referring to this period as the Age of Aquarius. However we choose to view this transition, humanity is awakening. Most of us have a sense that something big is on the horizon.

Reincarnation And The Cyclical Nature Of Life

Reincarnation is the belief in the rebirthing of one's spirit after death. This is mentioned throughout ancient texts and in spiritual ceremonies touching on many of the world's religions including Kabbalistic Judaism, Hinduism, Buddhism, Taoism, Jainism, Sikhism, Rosicrucianism, Theosophy, Greek Platonism, and Wiccanism. Ancient Egyptians viewed death as an initiation to move from one level of being towards a higher state of being. "Upon the death of a human being, the soul is really transferred to another living creature and becomes manifest in the world again."[53]

I became a believer in reincarnation preceding a couple of extraterrestrial visitations, in which several of my past lives were revealed to me. During these experiences, my consciousness left my present awareness and I was plopped into some other moment in time where I relived some of the most striking moments from previous lives.

My Native American Life

In one of my passed lives, I was as an impoverished, Native American woman, who lived in a tiny shack with dirt floors. My husband, or significant other, whom I loved and admired very much, was the Shaman and Spiritual Storyteller of our tribe. He was well respected for keeping our sacred stories and rituals alive.

Poverty entrapped us to no end. We wanted to continue to live off the land, as we had survived this way for generations, but the

European settlers sent their soldiers and government officials into our lives who forced us to live differently. We lost our freedom and we developed a love-hate relationship with the white man, who would frequent our reservation, bringing us food, blankets, medicine and other goods when we were in need. They used bribery and trickery, and took away our spirits (as we would say), because they never gave anything from their hearts. They always had an agenda with every visit. Sadly, the more they interacted with us, the more we became increasingly dependent on them to take care of us, until one day, we forgot how to take care of ourselves.

Tragically, one of the things the white man shared with us was alcohol – and lots of it. My incredible husband, whom I loved dearly, began to drink large quantities of the alcohol every day. At first, we thought the alcohol could be used to connect us more deeply to the spiritual realms. We thought the alcohol could help us enter into an altered state of consciousness during our ceremonies like some of the natural plants provided. However, we soon discovered that alcohol was different. It often made us sick, disconnected, and our ceremonies were sometimes interrupted by the disruptive nature of this new drug that the white soldiers were bringing to our tribe.

My husband became addicted to the alcohol, because he drank and drank and drank, until he was no longer capable of raising a family with me. I sent my children to be raised by my mother, so I rarely saw my own children. I was sad and angry at my husband for doing this to us, but it was not his fault. I was mostly sad that as a Native American tribe, we were losing our ways.

One evening, a soldier came to our door with a wool blanket tucked under his arm along with a wooden crate filled with bottles of liquor. The gift of alcohol, blankets, clothing, and food was often given in exchange for our land and our souls, and it was destroying us. My husband, who was in a drunken state, opened the door to the solider and began yelling at him, while attempting to push the soldier away from the door.

He told the unwelcomed intruder, "Leave and don't come back. We no longer want anymore of your things!"

Our tribe was growing weary of the repression, as our spiritual, mental, and physical well-being continued to decline. My husband turned away from the soldier to walk back inside and was shot from behind. He fell to the floor, and the dead of night permeated the air, beckoning a type of silence I will never forget.

Without saying a word, the soldier set the blanket and crate down by the entrance of our house, mounted his horse, and galloped into the dark hills of the night as if nothing had happened. I was bewildered, as I stood over my husband's lifeless body.

I continued to experience more memories from several past lives, until I began to see how karma was playing itself out in my current life. There was definitely a bigger picture and a connection that my past lives had influenced on my current life.

I discovered that I have been repeatedly reincarnating with a soul group or soul family, which is when close family members or friends from a previous life choose to reincarnate together again. If there is any past karma that needs to be worked out, then incarnating with these same loved ones again can complete and balance a life story, especially if the previous life didn't end very positively or if there was unfinished business that needed to be worked out. My husband from the Native American life returned to be my best friend in this life. This is the same soul; but in this life, she chose to incarnate as a woman.

Barbara, my life-long friend in this life, kept many of the same traits from the Native American life. In fact, those who meet her often think she is a Native American, although she has no Native American heritage in this life. She has always had an affinity for Native American artwork and artifacts, horses, and the Sedona Arizona area.

Karma has shown up for her in this lifetime too, as it does for all of us who incarnate again. Barbara experienced a difficult childhood and was raised in poverty with an alcoholic father. She was the eldest of nine children, so she naturally took on the role of being the family caretaker.

When Barbara was in her teens, her mother released her and her siblings to the care of foster homes, because there simply was not enough money to feed and care for nine children, and the dysfunctions that resulted from her father's alcoholism compounded the problems. Ironically, this life situation for Barbara was similar to what happened to the children whom she fathered in her previous life. The difference is that Barbara learned a great deal about the effects that alcoholism has on children, when experiencing it from this perspective.

Just like Barbara, my father in my present life, was also drawn to Native American artifacts and to the Sedona Arizona desert, which is where he retired. The past life memories helped me recognize that my father in this life was my uncle in the previous life, who was the chief of our tribe. I was very bitter when he became the chief, and had feelings of anger, resentment, and jealousy. I felt that my father in that life should have earned the status of being chief, instead of my uncle. I don't recall all the reasons why, but I had issues with my uncle that I just couldn't get past – so karma played itself out. My uncle at that time, incarnated as my father in my current life, so we could work out our differences. Whatever we despise or push away becomes our karma, because all emotional energy always finds its way back to its rightful owner – regardless of whether the energy is positive or negative.

As I was growing up, my father and I had a volatile, bittersweet relationship. I adored my father, but I also found him to be stubborn and arrogant at times, just like he was in the previous life. Now, I had to deal with these feelings up close and personal, as we played out the roles in our father-daughter relationship.

He and I had some rocky times, but a more unconditional loving bond grew out of the relationship we shared in this lifetime. Because of the latest incarnation we shared, we were able to redo some of the familiar patterns from the previous life and work out any issues. At the time of my father's passing, there was closure ending with unconditional love, forgiveness, peace, and understanding, as opposed to the previous life, where we departed with feelings of unresolved bitterness.

The role of karma is very important, because it is the thread that nourishes our soul so we can learn, grow, ascend, and become more enlightened than we were before. We are the force behind the action that karma takes in our lives. We are the co-creators in our lives and the universe is our magic slate. Whatever we express with our heartfelt emotions and intentions will manifest as karma somewhere, sometime, and someplace.

Neither my uncle nor my husband, from the Native American life, were blood relatives; but all three of us lived in the same tribe during that incarnation. My uncle and husband did not have any unresolved issues with one another, so they didn't have a need to share in a relationship when they incarnated in this lifetime. However, at one point in time, I introduced my father to my friend, Barbara, and I found it interesting as I watched them get acquainted (or reacquainted) with one another.

They both recognized each other as they gazed at one another, perplexed, trying to identify "where" or "how" they must have met previously? They went through their life events trying to find out where they may have crossed paths, addressing places where they worked, the cities they lived in, the schools they went to, and they talked about their interests. They could not figure out their connection.

I later told them about my past life memories and the role each of them played in the Native American life. Neither one of them had conscious memory like I did, but a feeling of resonance was definitely a reality for both of them.

The Laws Of Karma

Karma serves as a mirror, reflecting back the energy that we've expelled out into the universe from our thoughts and emotions. The stronger our emotional reaction to any situation, the more powerful the energetic frequency will be that we expel outward, whether positive or negative.

The more love, passion and gratitude we feel and "express", the more this same energetic vibration will be reflected back to us, because energy literally finds its way home to its original owner. You reap what you sow. This concept is based on the simple laws of physics. What goes out must come back.

Karma is not judgmental. It simply is the manifestation of cause and effect, stemming from emotional energy. The closer you are in a relationship with someone, the more frequently you will experience strong emotions surrounding certain situations. It is our emotions that cause the karma, and this is especially noticeable when we emit negative emotions like jealousy, anger, hatred, or sorrow. Emotions are energetic. Your heart chakra is your emotional center where this energy powers through, so what you think and feel will always manifest somewhere.

Your heartfelt emotions manifest as intentions that take action, whether this is through loving actions such as by being of service to others, or whether the actions are spiteful, causing chaos and disharmony. All actions will be reflected in the relationships you have with other people, because people serve as the mirror where karma's energy can play itself out.

Again, there is no judgment – only cause and effect. Your heart is constantly sending powerful blasts of energy out into the universe. This energy will always find its way back to you, because that energy belongs to you. The more positive choices you make in your life that bring peace and harmony to yourself and others, the more you will start seeing these same results appearing in your everyday life.

If we understand that the universe is alive and it stores every bit of information that we put into it, and if we also compare the function of the universe to be similar to the way the physical body operates, then we can see that homeostasis is always the end goal. Karma is nothing other than the interdependent webbing of energy within the universe that constantly repatterns itself to maintain homeostasis and balance.

These energetic patterns are invisible, but nonetheless, we can better understand this when we look at the interwoven pattern of a spider's web. For illustration purposes, suppose the center point of the spider's web (Fig-13) is representative of your point in consciousness. The circular arc lines (A) around the center of the spider's web represent the timelines reflective of one's level of consciousness. The straight lines that branch away from the center provide opportunities to climb the ladder of ascension.

There are crossroads or learning opportunities throughout life that are representative of the intersection points on the spider's web, where you can either climb up to the next level in ascension or you can stay in your current timeline or level of consciousness. We have all had experiences where we seem to repeat the same negative experiences over again; until we finally grasp the lessons we are supposed to learn. Only then, can we move on.

The circular time loops, between each ascension line, provide us with opportunities to relive similar experiences that are similar in vibration. Once we learn what we need from those sets of experiences, we are ready to move onto the next level in the

ascension of our consciousness.
opportune

(Figure-13)

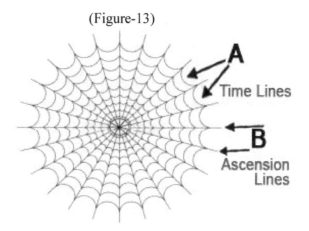

The closer you are to the center of the spider's web, the more opportunities there are for learning and growth, because there are more opportunities to jump on the ascension lines, since the intersection points are closer together. Difficulties may present themselves more frequently, providing you with powerful lessons so you can move outward to the next set of timelines that are higher in vibration. As you ascend along the straight ascension line (B), the circular time lines in the spider's web (A) become further apart or more spread out. This means there will be fewer challenges the further you ascend spiritually.

Your lessons are always going to be a vibrational match to the particular time loop that your ascension lines intersect with, which is why we have heard that we are never given more than we can handle. You won't stay in that same vibration or in the same group of time lines once you have learned the types of things that are associated within that vibration.

If we magnify the spider's web to be as large as we can imagine, there would be an infinite number of timelines and ascension lines that could expand out as probabilities. Where you travel along your ascension timeline depends on your choices, perceptions, and emotional responses.

Scientists suggest there is a strong possibility that we live in a multiverse that stretches out into infinity, creating a patchwork quilt of infinite parallel universes that our consciousness is constantly shifting in and out of, as we move through our perception of time. [54]

The challenges you are faced with today are necessary to bring you towards the next level in your ascension. The fastest way to evolve from one ascension point to the next is to maintain a positive and loving attitude, no matter what comes your way. Always emit only the highest emotional vibration from your heart and set your intentions to notice the positive side in everything. This is the fastest way to align with those timelines that match a higher frequency.

Feeling Stuck

We have all had the experience of feeling stuck at some point in our lives. Examples of feeling stuck might be when you find yourself dating abusive boyfriends or girlfriends repeatedly but can't seem to figure out why you have been unable to meet someone who treats you with love and respect. Or, perhaps you find yourself going from one job to the next only to continue to find employers that are oppressive or don't pay well enough to meet your basic needs. You might be attracting situations in your life that challenge you to stand up for yourself. Most often these lessons are about self-love and self-respect. Whatever the situation or lesson, once you figure out how to master whatever oppresses you, then the karma cycle for this particular event will stop looping.

You may not be conscious of what caused you to become "stuck" in the first place or when you actually became "unstuck", but the reality is, feeling stuck is an intuitive experience that results from wanting to move out of an existing vibrational time loop. It can be challenging to know what the lesson is for the next level of ascension, but once you find it and make the shift in your thinking, actions, and intentions, then you can ascend out of any particular time cycle you are in. Once you do, the feeling of being stuck melts away, because you literally shift into another parallel reality within a completely different vibrational frequency.

Ancient Knowledge Of The Spider's Web

Our ancient ancestors understood that the design of the cosmos was much like the weaving of a spider's web. According to Native American legend, a Spider Woman or Grandmother Spider lived in the sky where she spun a giant web to create an interconnecting web of life. The dew on the web became 7 shining stars. The first thoughts of universal mind were formed from her web and all living things remained connected to this same web. We are never alone, because we will always remain connected to her web through an invisible cord of energy. The cord allows us to experience our senses while dwelling in our physical existence, develop intuitive spiritual wisdom, and remain connected to our creator.[55]

The myths and folklore retold over thousands of years by our ancient ancestors may not be so mythological after all. The description of Indra's Net and the reflecting jewels parallels quantum theory in that our universe is a hologram.

"Far away in the heavenly abode of the great god Indra, there is a wonderful net which has been hung by some cunning artificer in such a manner that it stretches out infinitely in all directions. In accordance with the extravagant tastes of deities, the artificer has hung a single glittering jewel in each 'eye' of the net, and since the net itself is infinite in dimension, the jewels are infinite in number. There hang the jewels, glittering like stars in the first magnitude, a wonderful sight to behold. If we now arbitrarily select one of these jewels for inspection and look closely at it, we will discover that in its polished surface there are reflected all the other jewels in the net, infinite in number. Not only that, but each of the jewels reflected in this one jewel is also reflecting all the other jewels, so that there is an infinite reflecting process occurring." [56]

British philosopher, author, and spiritualist, Alan Watts is known for the following quote:

"Imagine a multidimensional spider's web in the early morning covered with dew drops. And every dew drop contains the reflection of all the other dew drops. And, in each reflected dew drop, the reflections of all the other dew drops in that reflection. And so ad infinitum. That is the Buddhist conception of the universe in an image."
– Alan Watts

Although we can't see energetic patterns with our naked eye, scientists know that the universe is put together mathematically and that our thoughts and emotions are energetic. The appearance of chaos or randomness is just an illusion out of our inability to see a connection, because nothing exists in a vacuum or outside of creation. Everything is always interconnected. The spider's web illustrates the way consciousness is interwoven within a universal grid, as a pattern, or as a fractalized component of the whole. This spider's web analogy has been shared among spiritualists, scientists, and our ancient ancestors alike.

Your Choices Today Effect Your Future Timelines

Every choice you have made in your past or that you will make in your future stems from a place of love and connection, or it stems from a place of separation and disconnection. Making choices from a place of love means that you are just as kind and loving towards yourself as you are towards others. Loving yourself is what brings out your greatest qualities. Being self-sacrificing, by pleasing others at your expense, or by disregarding your feelings or beliefs in order to accommodate another person is not operating from a place of love. You cannot give your best to others if you are self-sacrificing or self-destructive.

Whenever our choices cause us to feel separate and disconnected, we are no longer living in our truth. The truth is that we are all spiritual beings having a human experience, which means that we all come from the same source. When we find our connection to our soul, we will see a light inside of ourselves, which is the same light that pulses in every living thing. When we harm another person, we are harming ourselves. Likewise, when we harm ourselves, we are also harming others.

When we connect to the light that beams from within and realize this is the same light that emanates from everything, then we will see that we are all connected by this same light. This is the true nature of our spirit and our soul. By loving ourselves as fully as we can, we will find that we will also enjoy more meaningful, loving relationships with others.

My British Life

Preceding my Native American life, I lived as a British woman and was married to a British man. We were upper class merchants in the 1800's.

I remember the sound of our British language, the formal clothes we wore, and the architecture of our house and what our mercantile store looked like. I remember our two children, our butler, our nanny, but most importantly, I remember the strong negative emotions I felt that were carried over as karma in my consecutive lives.

I loved my husband dearly and we worked hard to maintain our lifestyle as well-known merchants. People from miles away arrived to our store by horse and buggy, as there were no cars during that time. Vendors would also come to deliver merchandise to our store, or my husband would take trips to meet with vendors and complete business transactions, as we continued to add more merchandise to our store. We sold a variety of things such as jewelry, knives, clothing, furs, flour, salt and other staples. We even baked and sold our own breads and sweets and I remember getting up very early each morning to tend to the kitchen along with our nanny, as we prepared and baked all the goods we would sell in the store that day.

We had two children – a daughter who was born first and then a son who was only a couple of years younger. The cultural formalities in how we raised our children were very different compared to how I have been raising my children in my current life. I was shaped by the extremes of gender and class division that was a prominent part of British culture at that time. As an upper class woman, I spent a great deal of time managing the affairs of my husband's business, which included baking, and sewing clothes to sell in our store, while our nanny tended to the children.

I had little interaction with my own children, but would occasionally call out to them by standing at the foot of our staircase and clapping my hands sharply two times, followed by the phrase, "chop chop". This would get their attention and they would briskly come down the stairs and I would inform them that dinner was being served or I would remind them to tend to their chores or studies. The children were expected to be subservient and well mannered, especially when being called to appear before any adults. Nurturing, hugging, or playing with children, wasn't something that upper class mothers did.

My husband's name was Roland and my name was Elizabeth. I remember the roles we played in that life with as much clarity as if it occurred yesterday.

I was a non-conformist in that life as I often express this same trait in my life today. I did not agree with the injustices that women were enduring at that time. I worked very hard along side my husband, and yet, I was always identified as *his property* or someone *less than* him. I was not a property owner, even though we were married and managed the store together. I was not allowed to express my own opinion, vote, have a discussion with other men, nor was I allowed to own and carry my own money. Everything belonged to my husband and although some women during that time accepted this to be the norm, it bothered me a great deal.

In order to feel like I had *something*, I decided to steal jewelry and other valuables from our store, which I hid from my husband. I thought that if my husband were to ever abandon me or pass away before me, I would finally, have something that I could call my own.

Little by little, I began hoarding merchandise from our store, stashing and burying valuables in a safe place. Of course, it didn't take my husband long to notice that his inventory was starting to go missing. I fabricated a story and told my husband that I witnessed one of our regular patrons stealing from us. My husband pretended to believe my story, but apparently he was on to me.

He said, "I hired a couple of detectives who I want you to talk with so you can tell your story to them. They will investigate this and then they will prosecute the man who you think is stealing from us." My husband proceeded to tell me that he setup a meeting place where I could meet with these two detectives so I could file a report with them.

I left by horse and buggy to go into another town the next day so I could meet the two men that my husband said were detectives. I walked into an empty building and sat on a cold, marble bench. The building was large and open, and I don't know what the building was used for. It may have been the lobby of an abandoned hotel or possibly an art museum. I sat alone inside the quiet building, waiting to be greeted by two men.

The men arrived and introduced themselves as detectives. They each wore a hat and a lengthier style coat and one of them carried a bag. They appeared to be official and looked like detectives. They each asked me a series of questions about the suspect who I claimed was the person stealing valuable merchandise from my husband's store. Then, one of the men asked me a question while he walked around behind me.

He asked, "Has the man who frequents your store ever walked up behind you like this?"

As the man walked behind me, he quickly draped a rope across the front of my neck, squeezing it tightly behind me, which forced me off the bench and onto the floor. The man continued to hold onto the rope while he knelt over the top of me, as I laid on the ground struggling for air. I could not breathe and this was how I experienced my death in that past life.

To this day, I cannot bear to have anything around my neck and I have never been able to wear turtlenecks without feeling very uncomfortable. I wasn't conscious as to why I felt this way until I became aware of this past life trauma.

After my death in that life, I witnessed several events that followed. Even though I was no longer living, I was aware that my husband sent our daughter to live with my sister. Our son remained at home and helped my husband run the store. My husband moved on and found another wife shortly after my death. Neither my husband or the two men were tried or prosecuted.

I remembered several other incidents from the British life throughout my late 20s and early 30s. I could not tell if any people from that life incarnated with me again until the age of 35, and then everything clicked.

In my current life, I met my second husband, Rainer at the age of 35. My soul recognized him the moment we met and I couldn't take my eyes off him, because the attraction I felt was so intense. I knew we had never crossed paths in this life prior to meeting one another, and yet, he seemed so familiar to me. There was a certain comfort that I felt deep inside my soul whenever we were in one another's presence. How could I know someone so well whom I had just met and how could I fall in love with someone so fast?

This was clearly more than a heightened level of hormones firing chemicals throughout my middle-aged body. I felt a certain bond between us that was already established even before we met.

As we became *reacquainted*, it didn't take long after Rainer and I moved in together when I realized that he was my husband, Roland, who I was married to in the British life. We had come back into each other's lives, once again, because there was unfinished business that we needed to work out.

After I recognized that Rainer was Roland, I noticed certain things about his character and personality that were carried over into this life, such as his desire to collect watches and his love for jewelry. As a merchant in the former life, he was quite attached to acquiring these types of possessions. One of his closest friends was a vendor of watches and jewelry. Roland and his vendor friend spent many long hours together talking at the store. Rainer's fondness for collecting watches today brings back comfortable soul memories surrounding his friendship in the previous lifetime.

Physical characteristics and mannerisms continued to present themselves in our relationship, helping me recognize that Rainer was Roland, but this was just the beginning. As soon as I learned about

Rainer's life history, and saw the way our lives unfolded together, I knew beyond a shadow of a doubt, that Rainer was indeed Roland, reincarnated.

When Rainer was 4 years old, he developed asthma and continued to suffer from this disease throughout his life. Could karma be responsible for causing Rainer to experience bouts of asthma? Rainer describes having intense fear and panic whenever he develops an asthma attack, because he feels like he cannot breathe. It is as if he is experiencing suffocation over and over again, as his soul tries to re-balance itself.

Prior to meeting Rainer, he recently went through a divorce, and for reasons unknown, Rainer's ex-wife forbade him from ever seeing his daughter again. Relatives reported that his ex-wife went so far as to tell their daughter in later years that her father was dead. Rainer took this matter to the justice system and parental visitation rights were granted, but his ex-wife and her entire family made it nearly impossible for Rainer to see his daughter. The ex-wife would either not show up during scheduled visitations, or her family would harass Rainer whenever he attempted to see his daughter.

Could it be that this negative life experience is in line with the law of karma once again? In the British life, Roland (now Rainer), sent his only daughter away to live with her aunt. He did not acknowledge the grief his daughter must have been feeling after her mother was murdered. In addition to grieving over the loss of her mother, she was abandoned by her father when she was forced to live with her aunt after her mother's death. Such experiences and trauma creates strong emotions like sadness, resentment, grief, and anger. Powerful emotions ignite the Heart Chakra's energetic output into motion, spiraling the law of karma into action.

Other interesting observations are that Rainer and I became merchants once again, only this time we succeeded in building and selling websites over the Internet. For the first time, I was able to enjoy business and property ownership as a woman, which was what I fought for in the previous British life. A large number of our clients also happen to reside in Great Britain. Another parallel is that I experienced several incidents of theft from a close friend whom I hired to work for me. I suffered a loss, not only monetarily, but I learned what the betrayal of someone's trust feels like, which is the greatest loss of all. In my opinion, karma was rebalancing itself once again.

There were many similar experiences that Rainer and I shared in both lives as karma played itself out. In this life together, we could experience the other side of what it feels like to be stolen from, what business ownership and equality or inequality feels like, what the experience of suffocation or strangulation feels like, and what it means to feel abandoned. This is all part of one giant learning process, which makes it possible to ascend towards higher consciousness. These events played out because of our soul's agreements, and because we are members of the same soul group.

When our soul passes into the afterlife, we each have a life review. The members of your soul group gather together and review any issues from your previous life along with you. Then, they collectively prepare for their next orchestrated story. The scripts are written. The roles that will be played are discussed. Those same souls are born again around the same time with one another, so they will share in each other's lives once again. Even though each soul incarnates into a new body with a new set of circumstances, this is really a continuation of the same soul's journey, as one story that continues to unfold into eternity. We are timeless beings learning and growing, as we climb towards oneness once again, which is where we originated.

CHAPTER SIX

YOU ARE CREATIVE

Dear One,

It's time to let go of any limiting beliefs you have about yourself and about the nature of the universe, so you can enter the zone of creative abundance, which knows no boundaries. Once you set yourself free from limitations, you can experience life as if it were a sea filled with endless possibilities and exciting new opportunities. You are expressing your creativity all the time, so it is important to become fully aware of "how" you are expressing your creative potential.

You hold a bright light within you and this light shines upon everything you come into contact with. How do you use this light within? Do you use your light to further enhance yourself and others in the most spiritual, joyful, expansive and passionate ways, or are you blocking your own light from shining, because you are adhering to a negative, limiting belief system?

Once you let go of fear, restrictions, or limiting ideas about yourself, which is the false sense of self, you will be connected to a higher vibration, which is linked to the infinite flow of creative, life-bearing energy. Creative energy is the fuel for your life and it is always centrally rooted in All That Is. Creation expresses itself through what it creates, and since you are an aspect of creation, then this means that you are a conduit for creation to express itself. Creation cannot exist without you and when you open the door to your own creativity, you will allow the light from All That IS to shine through you.

This creative light filters down into your physical body from your higher mind or from your higher self. It is the spark that gives life to your creations and manifestations. This light comes from the energetic field of All That Is, which is constantly creating, constantly vibrating, and constantly shining its light through you, so long as you allow it to do so.

This creative light cannot shine through you and do the work if you block it. As you become aware of the ways you have been blocking this creative energetic flow, this alone will allow the light to shine brighter, because truth and illumination are one and the same. This includes: Discovering the truth about who you are, the truth about the universe, and the truth about your own limitless potential. When you allow positive, creative energy to flow into your life, any obstacles that once weighed you down will dissolve, as though they never existed at all.

The transparency of this light will open up a channel that will bring you into full awareness of your higher self. Your higher self will no longer seem like it is something out of reach or something that only exists in your imagination. Your higher self is your true self and when you allow your true self to become illuminated and bathed in light – abundance and infinite possibilities will be part of your everyday experience. This is the real YOU, and you can choose to identify with your infinitely abundant birthright, and express creative manifestations anytime you want.

Every time you think of your higher self and see this version of yourself in your minds eye, you will come to know that you are a flawless aspect of creation. You are the creator in your own life and you are powerful, capable, and beautiful. There isn't anything about your higher self that you will ever need to change. Your higher self is a perfect creation and reflection of All That Is. When you embrace and allow this higher aspect of yourself to work through you, you will realize, that simultaneously, you are also letting go of the ego self, which is the false sense of self, and this is the only thing that has been holding you back.

Transcribed From:
The Voice of Creation

. . . .

"Life isn't about finding yourself. Life is about creating yourself."
– *George Bernard Shaw*

There are three words that explain how thoughts transform into creative manifestation. These three words are: Conceive; Perceive; and Receive. The acronym is CPR, which is the necessary formula that breathes life into anything you want to manifest.

Conceiving Your Ideas Or Imagined Inspirations

In order for anything you desire to manifest into physical reality, you first must "conceive" of the idea or welcome a creative thought into your mind. All creative thoughts or inspirations that excite and motivate you, come from your higher mind or higher self. Your ability to create is synonymous with creation.

By allowing your imagination to run free without restrictions, ideas will flow, providing you with inspirations that guide you towards manifestation. This is what will lead you to the greatest life you can imagine. All matter emanates from that which is conceived, so conceptualizing an idea is the first step within the laws of creation.

You cannot imagine what you do not already possess. In other words, the very fact that you can imagine anything about yourself means that this particular version of you already exists. Your imagination is your conscious ability to tap into parallel realities that exist at the same time as your physical reality. If you can imagine yourself as a blissful, happy person, surrounded by people who love you, and if you can see yourself radiating self-confidence, living abundantly, and all your needs are met, then these aspects of yourself already exist, or you would not be able to imagine them.

It is important to know that what you want to experience is not only possible, but it is also real and probable. The best way to turn dreams into reality is to believe in their potential, beyond any shadow of a doubt. This will allow you to tap into the parallel reality that you prefer.

All physical manifestations are a reflection of what you believe to be true and possible. If you don't believe in what you imagine or visualize, or if you think its manifestation isn't possible, then it simply won't come into being. That is how powerful you are. This leads us into the next stage of manifestation, which is "perceiving".

Perceiving Your Ideas Or Imagined Inspirations

Once you have "conceived" of an idea, the next step is to "perceive" the idea. This step transforms energy from one state into another, because in order to perceive anything, you must turn a thought into an emotion. Does the idea or thought excite you, make you feel alive, and enhance your current situation? If so, what do you intend to do with it? In this stage of manifestation, you will either positively embrace what you imagine, or you will discard it.

Unfortunately, many great ideas are discarded and dreams are never realized, because we allow our inner critic or the ego to put up roadblocks, based on our limited beliefs. This happens when you receive an inspiration and you tell yourself, "I don't think I can do that. It seems impossible!"

Alternately, you can welcome your fantasies and inner imaginings with openness and enthusiasm, just as you did when you were a child. A child's reality is positively enriched through their imaginative mind, until the child is taught otherwise. Children are naturally self-explorative and self-expressive because they allow their imagination to guide them. All we need to do is remember how we used our mind's eye when we were children. We did not criticize, belittle, or negatively label anything that came through our imagination. Instead, we allowed ourselves to remain open, joyful, and excited about every possibility.

When you perceive ideas as inspirations instead of impossibilities, you are moving energy from your mind's eye into your heart space. Emotions, like excitement, joy, love, and passion, are what give thoughts their power to manifest and crystalize. When you remain open to all possibilities, more ideas will flow to you that you can work with.

Positive or negative perceptions are the deciding factor that determine how much abundance you will allow into your life. It is like turning on a water faucet, and deciding how far you will crank the nozzle. Are you willing to let go of fear and limiting beliefs so you can allow your dreams and desires to flow to you? You have the free will to choose how you will perceive anything. Are you going to perceive inspirations and ideas positively, allowing them to grow, expand, and blossom, or will you squash your own dreams before they can manifest?

What you imagine as a possibility and what you believe is probable are not always congruent. In order to make a change in your life and manifest something, your beliefs must be in alignment with your imagination. To do this, simply choose to respond positively whenever you imagine something that brings you joy and excitement. When you dream the biggest dreams, simply believe in their possibility that they will manifest. This will shift your consciousness to move into a parallel reality that holds this same vibrational frequency, reflective of your confidence that things will work out as they are supposed to.

You are the only one who can decide what reality you wish to *become*, or come into. What becomes realized comes through the act of "perceiving" what you "conceived" or imagined to be true. If you want to experience more abundance, wisdom, love, and happiness, simply broaden your beliefs about what you think is possible. Know that you can have anything you can imagine, and more.

Receiving Your Idea Or Imagined Inspiration

The last step in the CPR of manifestation is to "receive" what you "perceive". Receiving something can only occur when you hold out your hand and welcome its manifestation. You must take physical action in order to receive something, and how you take action is always going to be based on your attitude towards your beliefs.

When you are inspired and excited about something, it is very easy to take action, but it can feel as though you are walking through mud if you try to act on something you are not excited about. Therefore, it is important to continue to follow the path towards your highest excitement and greatest joy. When you follow your dreams and inspirations and take them as far as you can, and act upon your bliss, you are naturally taking action to receive your manifestation.

You can feel confident that the manifestation has already been "received" in a parallel reality whenever you remain in a constant state of enthusiasm. Your consciousness will transition into the reality that is most in alignment with what you believe to be true and probable.

During the "receiving" phase, it is important to act with persistence when you are excited about something and ignore the external world as a means for measuring feedback about how things are unfolding. CPR is a creative process where you move energy from the fourth dimension into the third dimension, so your thoughts can crystalize and materialize. You are literally turning energy into matter.

It is crucial to maintain a positive attitude during this last phase of manifestation, regardless of what obstacles come your way. It takes time for everything to come together. You won't see a change in the external world immediately when you practice CPR, but when you continue to maintain a heightened level of enthusiasm and gratitude because you know that what you want already exists, then your physical reality will eventually match the state of your consciousness.

How you "conceive", "perceive", and "receive" your thoughts becomes your manifestation. You are manifesting all the time. Once you become consciously aware that every thought leads to a vibratory output, you can direct your thoughts to align positively with your beliefs and emotions, and this will reflect a close match to what you will actually experience in your physical reality.

Colonel Sanders, the founder of Kentucky Fried Chicken™, was forced to retire at the age of 65 after owning his own restaurant called Sanders Court & Café, because a new interstate was being built in his restaurant's location. His retirement was insufficient and he needed a job, so he decided to go door-to-door to other restaurants in search of a partner who would help him promote his chicken recipe.[57] He was rejected 1,009 times, mocked, and ridiculed for trying to sell his recipe, until Pete Harman of South Salt Lake, Utah agreed to partner with him. They launched the first Kentucky Fried Chicken™ restaurant in 1952. Within eight years, there were more than 600 franchised locations in the United States and Canada. Today, the franchise has 1,700 locations around the world.[58]

Although the external world was not immediately supportive of what Sanders "conceived", he did not allow this to determine his fate. He continued to practice CPR by "perceiving" and "receiving" his inspiration in the most positive ways. Eventually, the physical world *caught up* to his level of enthusiasm. The positive energy he continued to emit eventually crystalized to match this frequency.

When you are in the receiving phase, it is important to never give up, even though it appears that the physical world is not cooperating. You can perceive resistance as motivation, reminding you that you simply need to apply more persistence in your pursuits. Many people give up during this phase, because they allow the outside world to determine their fate, and rejection then becomes their projection. It doesn't have to be this way. You can always choose to stay in control of your manifestation.

We all have the ability to turn our own experiences into a Colonel Sanders success story, simply by practicing CPR. This is the formula for resuscitating dreams that you may not realize you have been blocking, because when you administer CPR, you are breathing life into what already exists. Since all probabilities already exist in parallel realities on the universal grid of consciousness, then you can take action and choose your spot on the grid. Whatever you want and desire already exists and is yours for the taking.

Play More Work Less

People are afraid to take action on their dreams, because they believe it will require a lot of 'blood, sweat, and tears'. The idea of working hard for something just to reach *a potential* outcome seems exhausting, so why even try?

We have been conditioned to associate the word "work" with something that is difficult, draining, and that requires commitment. The word "play" has the opposite meaning. Play is expansive and fills us with joy. Work and play are derived from the same source of energy, which is taking action towards manifestation, but "play" is positive, fun, and exciting. Work can make us feel oppressed and discouraged, so whenever you take action to reach any goal, it is helpful to *play* with the potential outcome. Stay flexible and joyous while you 'play with the clay' that molds every desire into physical existence.

Use your imagination. Fantasize and pretend you already have what you want. What does success feel like? When you have reached your dreams, what do the people and your surroundings look like in your imagination? These are the ways children use their imagination, which allows them to naturally connect to the fourth dimensional aspect of themselves.

Play is so energizing and exciting that children will cry if they are interrupted from it. We were all born with the ability to use our imagination and we can all tap into this powerful aspect of ourselves to manifest the life we truly desire.

Remember that when you play with the clay of imagination, the outcome does not need to be a perfect match to what you see in your mind's eye. Let go of expectations, but don't let go of dreaming big. Keep dreaming the biggest dreams you possibly can and allow your excitement to grow as big as it possibly can. Then, take this even further each day until your dreams and excitement feel as though you can't contain them any longer.

This creative energy will begin to take on a life of its own and it will want to be released out into the universe. You will feel called to take action when your dreams and emotions are in this state. Once you take action and breathe life into your dreams, sit back and enjoy whatever comes your way. When you remain flexible with the outcome, you will appreciate all the miracles that transpire, because creative energy is always filled with wonder and surprise.

It Always Starts With Imagination

It can be very relaxing to let your imagination run like an overflowing cup of water, as unfiltered ideas spring into your mind. You are the artist behind the canvas; capable of painting and creating whatever you want, but if you have a block in your belief system, this can block the flow of ideas that stream to you.

For example, if you believe you can only be happy *sometimes* or *during certain occasions*, then this is how you will experience happiness. If you believe that it is not possible to experience abundance all the time, then this will be your experience.

The surest way to manifest the life you want is to remove any obstacles. First, you have to think about what you want by imagining it. You have to respond positively to what you are imagining by believing in it. Finally, your emotions must be positive so when you take action, there isn't anything holding you back. Everything must be aligned positively, and then you will be able to take your dreams to the next level, which is actualizing them.

Do you prefer to be the happiest person you can imagine yourself to be, or do you prefer to be the sad and depressed person? If you look with your imagination, you are capable of seeing both versions of yourself. One is the parallel reality that will lead you to your higher self that exists in a higher vibration, and the other version of you exists in a lower vibration. You can choose the version of yourself you want to experience and *become*. Your imagination is your guide. You will BE whatever you COME to believe.

When you allow your imagination to show you the greatest joy and love you can possibly have for yourself, you are setting the stage to shift to the parallel reality where that version of YOU already exists. Why would you want to create any limitations when you can easily imagine something positive that is infinite in its raw form? There are no limits to imagination. When you clearly envision the person you want to be, see the career path or talents you want to pursue, and visualize all the ways that you want to BE in the world, your heart will respond with excitement, passion, and joy. The positive emotions that follow are what fuels thoughts into action, because with every beat of your heart, you are sending an electromagnetic vibration out into the universe.

Your heart is the communication center for the soul. When you experience feelings of love, passion, gratitude, excitement and confidence – this higher vibrational frequency binds to the closest parallel reality where a similar vibratory field exists so the manifestation can be experienced. Likewise, if you adhere to a limited belief system causing feelings of despair, depression, anger, or resentment, then your consciousness will become linked to a similar parallel reality that reflects this same vibration.

You are the creator of your conscious experience 100% of the time. To experience the best manifestation you possibly can, allow your inspirations and imaginings to be your guide, and follow your heart by doing only what you love to do and feel passionate about. If you do not love what you are doing and would rather be doing something else, it is important to choose differently.

When you let go of the fear that prevents you from doing what you love, you will raise your vibration, which will attract experiences that are more in alignment with what you truly desire. This is what will give you the manifestations of your dreams. No one is going to force you to do what you love. This is always up to you. Your higher self will guide you with inspirations and dreams through your imagination, but you always have the freedom to choose what you will do with this.

You have been manifesting your reality your whole life. The only difference is that you are now aware of a formula called CPR. Now that you know how creative energy flows, you can consciously channel your energy using CPR. You can live your life fully conscious of every manifestation, simply by becoming aware of your thoughts, feelings, and actions.

Turn Future Timelines Into Past Timelines To Impact Your Present Experience

You can achieve a future goal for yourself quicker and more efficiently when you visualize that the successful outcome has already occurred. Imagine that your goal has already been reached and feel those feelings of success right now. What you are essentially doing is manipulating your own timeline. You can imagine any desired future achievement and label it as a past experience simply by imagining that it has already occurred. When your perception about the past changes, your perception of the "now" also changes.

Time is only linear from the third dimensional perspective. You can influence your third dimensional time-space experience simply by manipulating your time-space experience from your fourth dimensional perspective, which is done by consciously manipulating your dreams, visions, and imagination. The third dimension is the materialization of energy, but your thoughts, intentions and emotions are energetic and fluid, and this is what you will always be able to direct with your consciousness.

When you imagine a desired future event occurring in a past timeline, you have merged your past and future timelines into one single moment. From your present perspective, you are in the middle of your success, and there is no other path you can take that exists outside of this. You are literally surrounding yourself with success!

You Are The Artist And The Art

You ARE what you create, so you are both the artist and the art. Creative expression is not only for painters, writers, or musicians, but every human being who is part of creation is a creative being. That includes you.

Talented artists and inventors remind us that we are capable of transforming imaginative thoughts into matter. Thoughts matter, which means that our thoughts have the ability to materialize – and where you focus your attention is where your energy will flow. What you believe and intend are the only things that matter enough to materialize, so it is important to choose your thoughts carefully so you will be proactive with pursuing only what you want, as opposed to attracting what you don't want.

You are constantly materializing something, because it is your nature to create. What you reap today is occurring because of what you believed in yesterday. You decided on the types of jobs you would be willing to do or not do. You decided on the types of relationships you believed you should or should not pursue. You decided on the type of home you would be willing to dwell in or not, as well as how you take care of yourself and express yourself everyday. Some of this was decided unconsciously, but nonetheless, your life is the reflective sum of your beliefs. Even if you choose to sit idly and do nothing – this is still a creative act that will manifest a particular outcome. Creativity is what births life into existence and creativity is what sustains life. As long as you exist, which is eternally, you will always create something.

When you pay close attention to your thoughts, beliefs and emotions, you will start to see that everything you experience in your outer world is a direct reflection of what you are experiencing in your inner world. To know this is true, take an inventory of yourself right now. Do you feel abundant, passionate, and excited about your life right now? Why or why not? If you aren't experiencing your highest excitement and your greatest joy right now, what belief do you have about obtaining this that is blocking you? You will find that when you think about it, the blockages are from your own belief system and not from some external force. Limitations are never based on any actual circumstances. Limitation can only be a perception that you apply as a definition to your experiences.

Circumstances are neutral until you apply meaning to them.

You are creating something everyday and in every way. You are the painter holding your own bucket of paint and you are either carelessly splashing paint all over the canvas, or your are focusing your attention on where you want your paint to go. You can create madness and chaos with your paint or you can create a world that has meaning and beauty. It all depends on whether or not you are paying attention to what and how you are painting. Nonetheless, you are always painting. You never stop painting. Every word, action, thought, emotion, behavior, and choice you make, is expressed by your paintbrush – and you are creating a world of art. This is your story. You can paint your story, write your story, tell your story, sing your story. Nonetheless, it is your story and you are the creator and always have been.

We often think that manifestation or practicing the laws of attraction only happens sometimes, but you are actually manifesting and creating all of the time. You are not only creating your reality all the time, but you are doing so in the most unique way. Every artist has their own style – their own way of creating. No one else is painting their world exactly like you are painting yours.

You hold a piece of the puzzle that exists within the map of creation. In order for your puzzle piece to fit where it needs to go, it is important that you paint your world according to how you want your world to be painted and not according to how someone else thinks you should paint it. In other words, if you try to bend for someone else in order to please that person or if you are painting your world the way you think others would like to see it, then you are changing your puzzle piece to be a different shape other than the way it was designed. You are doing a disservice to yourself and to others when you hold back from expressing who you are, because then your puzzle piece will not fit correctly within the overall scheme of creation. The most moving stories and the most beautiful works of art are original, born straight from of the heart of the artist. There is no duplication with authentic creation.

You are expressing your original creative nature in every moment of your existence. When you communicate and formulate words, you are creating your own original message that you are passing onto someone else. When you do your job at work, you are creating a special way in which you deliver the results of your accomplishment to others. If you bake a cake, you can share that same recipe with several people, but every cake is going to turn out slightly different. This is because every person has their own unique stamp on everything they do. When creative energy transmits through you, no one will do the same task in exactly the same way as you, no matter what it is that you do. You are unique because you are the product of creative energy, just as you are the transmitter of creative energy.

In order to become all you can be, it is important that you always operate from your personal truth. Your truth is not what someone else thinks you should be. Your truth is not based on the limitations set forth by your ego. Your truth is the light that emanates through you. We all have this light within us and how you choose to use your light is how you will define your truth.

When you set aside the limitations and artificial beliefs that your ego has prescribed to you, you will find your truth. When you press forward because you know that your intuition is your guide, even though you don't know exactly how things will turn out, then you are living in your truth. When you allow yourself to imagine and envision the greatest possible life for yourself, ensuring that what you imagine is also congruent with your beliefs about what you think is possible, then you are living in your truth.

What To Do When Your Beliefs Don't Match The Desires Of Your Heart And Soul

Your inner critic, the negative ego, and the hindering beliefs that go against your greatest potential are nontruths. You can choose to believe in these limiting labels, which aren't the real definition of your true self, or you can choose to discard them at any time.

When you can imagine and feel a greater life for yourself but you abstain from moving forward because you are listening to your inner critic who is telling you that something is not possible, then you are allowing your ego to be the dictator of your life. When this happens, you have the power to stop the negative self talk by simply asking yourself if this is what you want to believe and align with? You have the power to choose something more positive, that is more in alignment with your true self, and not in alignment with the ego's artificial self.

You have a higher, unlimited self that is not confined by boundaries. You can choose to live at one with creation and All That Is, by merging with the highest aspect of yourself, in which you will not experience any limitations or boundaries.

Your feelings are your compass. You will know whether or not you are operating from your higher self or from your negative ego, simply by the way you are feeling. If your emotional state is enthusiastic and positive, then you are allowing your higher self to be your guide. If your emotions reflect helplessness, anger, or fear, then you are operating from your ego.

When you catch yourself worrying about the future, remember that you can take charge of your future by focusing on the kind of future you want instead of worrying about what you don't want. You no longer need to accept that you are just a victim of the unknown. You can also remove dreadful feelings about the past by changing your perspective about the past. These techniques will align you with more positive timelines, and this will shift your current vibration so you will no longer operate from a limited belief system. Your authentic self will step in and become the driver of your destiny.

Let Nature Be Your Guide

When you observe the beauty of nature that surrounds you, and focus on blissful stillness, instead of listening to the mind's chatter, you will instantly shift your attention away from your ego and realign with your higher self. When you bring your awareness back to the "now", you will be in a position to simply observe the critical inner voice of the ego instead of reacting to it.

You can shift your focus in any moment to be one with nature. Whether you find yourself distracted by worries about the future, if you are dwelling on a hurtful past, or if you feel like you are stuck in a belief that is not serving you positively, take notice of the way new trees and plants sprout after an entire forest has been destroyed by a fire. Listen to birds singing by a bubbling creek; whispering trees rustling in the wind; and the roar of the ocean. Marvel in all the ways your body heals, repairs, and regenerates itself, as new cells constantly replace the old. You are always part of creation and All That Is.

There is no storm great enough to interfere with the ever flowing abundance that continues to unfold effortlessly in nature. There is no obstacle that does not also lead to a solution, whenever we observe nature.

Life has the ability to reproduce and renew itself during times when logically, this would seem impossible. It is because the creative life force is infinite and constant. Always there. Always creating. Always expanding. Creation and creativity will always find new ways to thrive. This is where the truth lies. Not in the limitations set forth by the ego mind or the inner critic.

You can let go of any belief that causes pain and suffering and replace it with something more positive. As a fractal of creation, you are a co-creator within the body of creation. There are no boundaries and there are no limitations within this framework. This is your true nature. Anything short of this awareness is constructed by your false negative ego, and this is a nontruth.

Once you realize that your ego has been the only limiting factor in your life, you can rise out of this darkness like the Phoenix rising from the ashes. Any perceived obstacles are nothing other than *perceived obstacles*. Your innate ability to create infinite abundance in your life is your true nature. There are no limits with creation, because in order for creation to exist, limitation cannot also exist. Creation is characterized by infinite, limitless possibilities, and overflowing abundance.

As a creative being, you have the ability to create or change anything you want, and this all starts within your mind. If you can imagine it or visualize it, then you can change and affect it. It's that simple. Whatever you want out of life, whether it is self-improvement, improving your finances, improving your relationships, finding solutions to problems, you will be able to create, manipulate, and influence all of these things, as you imagine them into existence.

You Can Change Your Past

In your present state of awareness, you can quiet your ego mind and silence the inner critic by simply connecting to nature, but what about changing those deeply rooted beliefs that you have acquired from your past that keep interfering with your daily life? Many people find that they are unable to move forward and accomplish their dreams, because a false belief system has followed them since childhood, or from past experiences. These limited beliefs about yourself may have come from your parents, your teachers, your friends, or from society.

It's time to pick up your paint bucket once again and realize that your paintbrush is in your hands and has always been in your hands. There is no one else painting your world other than you. This means that you are always shifting from one parallel universe to the next; based on whatever world you are painting for yourself at any given moment. When you paint your world, you are simultaneously creating your perceived past, present, and future, all within each brush stroke. Anything the artist creates is out of the perception of the artist. There is no other reality other than what you perceive to be true.

If you believe you had a negative past or that something in your past is holding you back, then you are choosing to bring this same belief into your present reality. You can create a new and different world for yourself in any moment. Simply choose not to bring the same past with you as you paint your current reality.

Just as you imagine your future and how you want it to look, you have the ability to imagine the same for your past. Who says you have to keep the same images alive again and again that are reflective of the same past? It's always your choice to perceive your past any way you want.

Whatever you believed in yesterday, does not need to be what you believe in today. Your imagination is unlimited and you can create a new set of desired circumstances that you can claim as your memories from the past. As you do this, you can create memories that are more reflective of who you are today instead of who you were yesterday.

For example, if you are holding onto a memory when a loved one hurt your feelings ten years ago, simply recreate that scene with your imagination and re-experience that moment to be loving and kind, in which the exchange did not hurt your feeling and did not affect you in the same way. In doing so, you will create a different past for yourself, which will be more congruent with the future you are also creating.

We have all heard that time heals all wounds. It is not that time heals any wounds. Your wounds heal when you've shifted into the parallel universes where you no longer feel wounded. You are always shifting to the parallel reality that is most reflective of your current belief system. The sooner you change your beliefs about how something affected you in the past, the faster your wounds will heal.

You don't need to wait for the passage of time to experience a healing. Simply change your beliefs and perceptions about the past and instantly, your emotional response will change, and this will affect your present state of consciousness. You don't have to allow negative beliefs about a troubled past hold you back.

In this moment you are a new person. In the next moment you will be a new person as well, because in every single moment, you are recreating yourself, as a brand new person. It appears as though you operate from the same perspective as you move through linear time; however, living with the same perceived history and the same dreams is a choice, even if it has been an unconscious one.

You can choose to operate from the same sets of beliefs, or you can choose to create what is more reflective of a past and future that you desire. You always get to decide who you will become. If you allow negative beliefs about a perceived past to define who you are today, then this is what you will keep creating over and over again.

When you imagine a different past for yourself, you are actually time traveling with your consciousness to a parallel reality where this alternate reality exists. There is no real past, because the past can only be *a perception* of what you think occurred. In fact, there is no presence of anything without the present, because you will always perceive the past from a present perspective.

If you don't like the way something looks or feels from your present point of view, allow yourself to change it. If you don't like the way your parents treated you when you were a child, then re-create scenes in your mind where you were treated differently. If you went through a bitter divorce, explore new ways to remember your divorce as being a peaceful separation instead of a devastating catastrophe.

At first, it may seem like thinking this way is not realistic, but when you trust the results from doing these imaginative exercises, you will discover that you have the ability to quantum leap into parallel realities where your old past is no longer part of your present experience. This is a shortcut towards experiencing any major transformation in your life, so you won't have to carry around so much pain and suffering. It does not need to take a long time to transform, heal, or obtain the future you've always wanted, unless you want your transformation to take a long time.

Working With Past Timelines To Change Your Present Circumstances

In certain situations, you can reimagine events from the past that will change the outcome of what you are experiencing in the present. For example, suppose you went to a party and drank too much alcohol or ate the wrong types of food, and you woke up feeling ill the next morning.

Instead of accepting the current status of "feeling terrible", you can change your present experience by reimagining a different past. To do this, simply revisit the party scene with your imagination. You can visualize drinking lots of water or enjoying a smoothie while you are at the party. You might observe yourself saying, "No thank you," whenever alcohol is being offered, and you can imagine yourself eating a healthy green salad instead of cake, chips, and fondue.

Even though there were no salads or smoothies served at the

party, your imagination can still visualize this. Your subconscious mind cannot differentiate fact from fiction, so your mind will convince your body that the other set of circumstances occurred, and your body will respond accordingly. I have healed food-induced stomachaches and headaches in an instant simply by doing these types of visualizations.

For even better results, you can adjust your intentions so your emotions match your thoughts. In other words, you can acknowledge that you made a poor choice and if you were to do it over again, you would make a different set of choices. It is important that you feel sincere about what you intended and desired. When you align your imagination and intentions with what you prefer, your current timeline will shift to a parallel universe that is more reflective of this new past.

What you remember to be true in your past will affect your present, no matter what it is. You can use this same technique to heal emotional wounds, fix misunderstandings, traumas, and within reason, you can turn poor choices into positive outcomes for your future. Your past is just as flexible and pliable as your future when you engage your imagination.

Changing Past Timelines To Heal Childhood Trauma

Manipulating past timelines to heal childhood trauma requires a slightly different technique. Sometimes the past is too painful to deal with, so we block those types of memories as a way of protecting the psyche. Childhood memories may also be difficult to interpret, because your perception as a child was different from what it is today.

When working with childhood timelines, it is helpful to think of these timelines in a more generalized way. For example, instead of recalling individual incidents from your memory, you can reflect on the feelings you experienced over larger blocks of time. For example, if you moved a lot before the age of six, you might have felt lonely from ages 3-6. Perhaps, your parents got divorced when you were seven. You may remember feeling angry and resentful towards a stepparent until the age of ten. At ages 11-15, you may remember feeling quiet and withdrawn. At ages 16-18 you felt fearless and invincible, while you engaged in some dangerous behavior. These are just examples about how you can work with blocks of time instead of individual incidents when healing childhood timelines.

One generalized way you can work with blocks of time is to think about each grade when you went to school. You can write down each grade along with a one-word adjective that most clearly defines your overall mood during that time. Below is an example of what this might look like this:

Kindergarten – Confused
First Grade – Insecure
Second Grade – Motivated
Third Grade – Withdrawn
Fourth Grade – Angry
Fifth Grade – Incapable
Sixth Grade – Talented
Seventh Grade – Insignificant
Eighth Grade – Smart
Ninth Grade – Afraid
Tenth Grade – Independent
Eleventh Grade – Happy
Twelfth Grade – Satisfied

If there are negative moods written next to specific blocks of time, you may be able to identify the parent, teacher, friend, or individual who hurt you, which led to the negative label. There may be more than one person that caused grief and anguish during a particular period of time.

When you manipulate the perceived events in your past timelines, you can begin to experience new relationships with all of those people. You will no longer need to hold onto animosity and resentment, because when you perceive your past through a new set of lenses, you are simultaneously experiencing a different timeline to label as your past.

We have the power to experience a different past that is more in alignment with what we prefer, the same way that we can imagine a different future for ourselves. Time is only linear when we remain in third dimensional consciousness, but when we expand our consciousness into the fourth dimension, we can draw up a new blueprint, creating what we prefer – regardless of whether we define this as past, present, or future. The fourth dimension holds the energetic blueprint to crystalize and manifest what we want into our third dimensional experience.

Of course you cannot change certain events that happened in the past if the events involved choices made by other people. For example, you can't bring the deceased back to life or change history as it was perceived by the masses, but you can change and effect your own timelines in the ways that the past affected you. Your newly defined past can reflect a version of yourself where your voice was heard, where you know you did the best you could, and where all outcomes ended peacefully, to your satisfaction. The way you deal with your past, defines who you are today.

How To Create A New Past Timeline

Once you have identified the person or persons from your past that led to any unpleasant memories affecting you today, simply set the intention to recreate the past. Find a quiet place, free of distraction, and allow yourself to have an imaginary encounter with the person or persons from your past. This can be done any way you want, as long as you create the encounter to unfold the way you desire.

Allow your imagination to paint a new scene on your canvas that is more positive and in alignment with the past you truly want. You can change the scenery surrounding the memory. You can change the reactions and responses between you and the other person. You can change the ages or timeframe when you want this revised event to occur. You literally have the power to change anything surrounding the past when you work with your imagination.

Your imagination is infinitely creative, so why not create the most loving encounter you possibly can with another person from your past? What would this look like in your minds eye? When you reimagine something positively, notice how animosity and resentment melt away, leaving you with feelings of love and unity once again.

If you have the ability to imagine a kinder more loving version of the person who hurt you, then there is a version of this person already in existence in a parallel reality. You have the ability to tap into this parallel reality; otherwise your imagination would not be able to perceive it.

Once you choose a new set of responses pertaining your past, you can set the intention that this is the new reality you prefer. Imagine a line drawn from your new past experience connecting you to your present timeline. Any surrounding events will also be influenced and affected by this change. This is how your past creates your present reality. You don't have to carry the same perceived experience of the past with you in every moment. You can bring lighter, more pleasant memories into your present awareness.

If you experienced a lot of shame and guilt as a child or if you are currently experiencing this in a present relationship with someone, you can imagine that you are placing shame and guilt into a box. You can wrap up the box like a present and kindly give it back to the person who gave it to you. During your imaginary encounter, you can say, "I have received this shame and guilt from you. I am not sure why you presented this to me, but it is not mine to own. I did not ask you for it and I do not wish to own it, so I am giving it back to you now."

Imagine yourself handing back this box of energy called shame and guilt, wrapped up as a present. When you give something as a gift, it is nearly impossible to attach feelings of anger and resentment when you release and let go of this energy. You will provide the other person with the opportunity to take responsibility for his or her own energy, and you will become free from that which wasn't your property in the first place. You do not have to physically be present with the person who hurt you in order to forgive that person. You don't have to talk it out, say you're sorry, or feel guilty when you practice forgiveness. Practicing forgiveness is a form of spiritual alchemy, which is an ethereal practice and not something that needs to be played out physically.

Forgiveness is always about giving back energy that does not belong to you. When you do this, you are transmuting dense energy and turning it back into love. All you need to do is operate from a loving heart. Whenever you turn dense energy or darkness into light and love, you are operating as a "Lightworker".

As long as you are part of the human experience, you are going to have times where you have hurt others or others have hurt you, because human beings are constantly expressing and experiencing a range of different energies, which vary in their densities. We are creative beings. We are made from energy and we co-create energy in all of our experiences, so there will be times when you will be dealt energy that causes pain, grief, or suffering.

Since energy is not visible to the naked eye, we are normally not aware when we take on another person's unwanted energy, nor are we aware that we do not have to continue to carry energy that we don't want to own. If we find ourselves carrying energy that is denser than we want to experience, we always have the power to transform it into light.

If you find yourself feeling tired, depressed, angry, or bogged down by lower vibrating energy, you can willfully transform that energy into a density you prefer. This will raise your vibration and the vibration of those around you. Your emotional state is the indicator or the barometer for the type of energy you are carrying.

In order to experience negative energy you have to label something as 'negative', by perceiving or interpreting an experience in this way. Someone cannot 'do' something 'to' you. Someone cannot 'make you feel' a certain way. People are responsible for their own feelings and actions, just as you are. We always have the free will to decide what we will hold onto or let go of, based on what we believe to be true. If you perceive another person's negative judgment about you to be false, then you won't take on their projected energy, because it won't apply to your belief system.

Loving Yourself Through It All

We gather information about how we feel about ourselves from the time we are children, based on how we think others perceive us. The feedback we receive from our parents, siblings, friends, teachers, neighbors, and society, shapes our views and how we define ourselves. If people responded lovingly towards us, we grew into adults who felt good about ourselves, for the most part. If the love we received was conditional and didn't meet our needs, we may find it difficult to know how to fully love ourselves. We might seek self-love through addictions, manipulation, or self-loathing.

The seat of the soul is pure love. We are born with this perfect loving condition, but as we grow into adults, we aren't always taught how to embrace our loving nature. We later find ourselves filled with self-hatred and we often do things that are self-destructive.

Rather than staying true to ourselves, we learn how to be someone we're not and we strive to please other people in order to feel that we are lovable or worthy of being loved. We are discouraged from looking in the mirror and fully loving ourselves just as we are. We are taught that it is more humble to criticize ourselves, find flaws and imperfections, and tear ourselves down, than to simply love ourselves as we are.

You are a fractal of creation and creation itself is infinite. There are no mistakes in creation, because the real definition of creation is that it has the ability to express itself in any way, shape, form, design and style that it possibly can. Creation never stops expressing and re-creating itself.

If you believe you are flawed, you will miss the opportunity to experience your life as fully as you can, because seeking perfection is not something that can ever be achieved. Perfection does not exist. It is merely a subjective idea that can only be measured against someone else's terms of what they believe is perfect.

The real meaning of perfection is synonymous with creation. Anything and everything that can possibly be expressed is already being expressed beautifully and perfectly within the full body of creation. There are no limits and no boundaries in creation. There can be nothing more perfect than this, and you get to be part of this. You are unique and there isn't anyone anywhere that is exactly like you.

All the pieces in your life had to fit together perfectly to bring you to this moment where you are today. You have the power to create your "now" experience to be anything you want, because you are a co-creator, existing as a puzzle piece in creation. You don't need to do anything or prove anything to someone else in order to fit your puzzle piece into the body of creation. You are perfect simply because you exist as a creative, sentient being.

When you allow yourself to be free from shame, guilt, and fear, as you express yourself freely, and when you live as fully as you can in every moment, this will lead you towards the greatest expression of "peicefulness" that there is. When you are your true self, all the other puzzle pieces in creation fit together, exactly as they were designed. The word "piecefulness" becomes "peacefulness".

Real peace comes from knowing you are whole. Experiencing wholeness comes from being free to embrace your individuality and uniqueness, and to do so without judgment or criticism. You are the only one who has the power to bring this forth.

CHAPTER SEVEN

YOU ARE LOVE

Dear One,

That which you call language, spoken by the tongue and heard with the ears, is not the only type of language that exists. There is another type of language that comes through the heart. This "heart language" is the language of the soul and the soul's language is always compassionate, loving, and connected to All That Is.

When you listen and communicate from your heart, you will bypass the limiting filters of your ego mind, and this will open up the channels for the divine mind to connect to you. All you need to do is "intend" to have a heart connection, and your intention will shift your focus away from the ego mind, and this will open up your heart center.

When you are heart centered, all communication will flow to and from your heart. You will receive information from a higher mind, because that is the only mind that influences the heart. You will also transmit information to others in this same way, because your highest truth will always come from the heart.

When you are not heart centered, communication from other people or from spirit will always be filtered by the ego. Your ego is the inner critic that manipulates the truth to match its own set of false beliefs.

Allow your heart to be overfilled with expressions of love and compassion. Invite cosmic knowledge and intuition into your heart. This will always be like a gentle wind, sweeping through you, unbiased and nonjudgmental – spoken from one heart to another. This is the how you will hear the language of love from The Voice of Creation.

Transcribed From:
The Voice of Creation

. . . .

"Just imagine becoming the way you used to be as a very young child, before you understood the meaning of any word, before opinions took over your mind. The real you is loving, joyful, and free. The real you is just like a flower, just like the wind, just like the ocean, just like the sun." – *Miguel Angel Ruiz*

A bee does not have to be taught or told how to be a bee and a tree does not have to be shown how to grow and stretch towards the sky. The vastness of life that extends throughout the world and throughout the entire universe, no matter how large or small, expresses its beauty in its own unique way. Beauty does not result from having to 'do' anything. Beauty is a state of being.

When we define something as beautiful, whether observing nature or another human being, we are seeing and connecting to something for which there are no words. We become speechless, awestruck, and explore the depths of our own inner silence. We become mesmerized and enamored by the presence of beauty, because we are wired to discover and appreciate its essence, whether it's from a mountain range, a flower, a painting, or when spending time with someone we love.

Seeing something beautiful results when we use our eyes to connect to the vibratory energetic field of love that is present in All That Is. The energetic vibration we call 'beautiful' that's capture with our eyes, is the same energy called 'love' that is felt in the heart. This energy is present in all things and we can perceive it in many different ways.

When you 'see' beauty and 'feel' love, you are tapping into the highest vibratory state that exists. This is the state where creation occurs, where miracles happen, and where your higher self resides. The more you allow yourself to connect to this state, the faster you will ascend and grow spiritually.

You Were Created From The Vibratory Frequency Of Love

You are a perfect expression of love. You cannot exist without love and love cannot exist without you, because you are part of the body of creation. Love is required in order for life to exist and thrive. A baby will die in the absence of love, physical contact, and care. That which makes us feel connected, expansive, joyful, compassionate, and united, gives us the emotional experience we call love. Love is constant and exists within us, outside of us, and it connects us to All That Is. All we need to do is take notice of it in order to experience it.

If love is a necessary part of our existence and it's always there, why do we often feel eluded by love? During stressful times, it may seem like we are alone and that love has abandoned us. We sometimes feel heartbroken, confused, or that life had betrayed us, but it is through our triumphs over the most difficult experiences, when we discover the greatest opportunities to connect with other people and build stronger bonds with one another. When you shine light in a dark room, you can see the light much more easily compared to looking for light in a room that is already filled with light.

Since love is an energetic frequency that never leaves us, because we were created out of love, we sometimes need to experience the opposing, darker side of life to be able to see love more clearly. An invisible thread connects us all and in order to return to our oneness and wholeness, which is where we originated from, we have to ride through some darkness and experience polarity.

If you don't know what separation is, how can you know unification? If you don't experience any fear, how can you learn how to find inner peace and strength? If you don't know rejection, how can you learn perseverance and self-love?

Flowers and trees are frequently beaten down by wind and rain, and we experience the same when a storm moves through our lives. In spite of the harshness of the storm, the flowers and trees still need the rain in order to thrive and grow. The wind purifies the air and carries seeds to new destinations, so new plants can sprout where they never existed before.

Our soul needs the variety of experiences that come through the eye of the storm, even though we don't like to get wet or feel beaten down. The discomforts are only temporary, but the nourishment the soul needs to grow, is permanent. After the storm dies down, flowers bloom, and trees become more lush and green. None of this would be possible without wind and rain.

The discomforts we experience in life are always just temporary and minor compared to what we will gain in the aftermath. When you remember this bigger picture no matter what comes your way, and when you identify love and oneness residing in everyone and in everything, you will be putting on a suit of armor, so you won't feel so weathered every time there is a storm.

Regardless of any outside circumstances or how dark the darkness seems, we can find an abundance of love everywhere and in everything. If we focus on feeling separate, detached, or unloved, we will simply not notice our connection to the vibration of love. It is not that love has eluded us or that it is not there. We simply won't see it when we are focused on the opposite – which is lack and separation.

As soon as we shift our awareness and remember our oneness with All That Is, and when we seek the goodness in every situation, we will realign with this natural state of being. Love always exists, regardless of what we choose to focus on, because we cannot exist without it.

Staying Heart Centered

When we feel love for another person, a pet, or even an object we are fond of, we know that this experience is always felt in the heart. Our heart is the portal where we interpret, experience, and express all feelings of love. The language of the heart is love, and love can be spoken in many different ways and through many different means, but regardless of the way it is delivered, it is always nonjudgmental, accepting, open, welcoming, and it is infinitely giving and expansive.

The communication of love between people is just as vast as the energy of love itself. Our life experiences provide us with countless ways and opportunities to express and deliver our message of love out into the world.

Our expression of love can be as simple as saying hello to a stranger, to being romantic and intimate with our partner. We love ourselves when we set boundaries when we need to, or when we simply draw ourselves a bath at the end of the day. We are constantly expressing love and recreating this life force energy within the fabric of our lives everyday.

Once we take notice that we are living from one loving moment to another, we will start to see that there has been an invisible vibration of love, existing as an undercurrent in everything we do, everything we feel, and in everything we see. A current of love exists within the root of every exchange, in every breath, in every prayer, in every smile, and in every tear.

When we know that the vibration of love exists in everything and never leaves us, we can stay connected to this vibration even when another person reacts in anger, jealousy, or haste. You can remain calm and aware that there is an invisible thread of love, which remains alive as vibrating energy between you and an opposing individual.

Even in the worst moments, there is still love, because without love, there would be no life. Love never ceases to exist. As long as you see life before your eyes, even if you don't agree with the choices someone else has made, love is still the vibrating current that exists in all of creation. Therefore, at the root of everything, you will always be able to find love, as long as you choose to see it.

The Language Of Love Is Harmonious And Synchronistic

Language is the means by which information is exchanged and there are many ways that language is communicated. Sometimes we communicate in words. Other times it is through symbols, emotional expressions, body language, written language, or music.

The language of love knows no boundaries. It can be expressed in an infinite number of ways and in any form you can imagine. When you become aware of the vast number of ways that love is being expressed through your interactions with other people and through your connection to the universe, you will be able to receive a deeper form of communication that only love can offer.

There are symbols and synchronistic events that occur in our life experiences designed to help us stay connected to the vibration of love, so that we will remember what is really important. I first became aware of the majestic nature of synchronicities during the summer of 2012. I decided to do some research on the Internet about the ending of the Mayan Long Count Calendar, that was fast approaching, in an effort to uncover any information about what the ancient Mayans were thinking when they ended their calendar on December 21, 2012.

In the midst of my research, I stumbled upon an article on a website about people who were witnessing strange synchronistic events, which seemed to be mirroring something within their own consciousness. People from all over the world were suddenly taking notice that they were seeing the same doubling of numbers appearing to them again and again.

The most common report was that people were repeatedly seeing the number 11:11, which was appearing to them everywhere – on the clock, when they happened to glance at the time, on their receipts, on their bank statements, on license plates, among other places. No matter what these people were doing, 11:11 continued to show up in their lives, and often during moments where one was having an epiphany or when one was simultaneously noticing that an expanded awareness was taking place. It was as if there was some kind of message encoded in the double number that said, "Pay attention to this moment."

What I found most amazing was that while I was reading an article about 11:11 synchronicities, I happened to glance at the clock on my computer monitor and the time was 11:11am. I knew the odds were too great for this to be a coincidence. This was not something I could have planned. Even though I wasn't sure why this happened, the synchronistic experience prompted me to pay closer attention to the frequency that this number was appearing in my life.

From that point forward, I began to see the number 11:11 nearly everyday. I was not someone who watched the clock. I was much too busy to wait idly for the time 11:11 to present itself. Nonetheless, in my busiest moments, I happened to glance at the clock during the precise time of 11:11, both morning and night, and I continued to see 11:11 appear regularly for about a year or longer.

Suddenly, my regular encounters with 11:11 nearly came to an end and this was replaced with new sets of numbers: 2:22 and 3:33. The frequency of seeing these new number pairs started happening as often as I had been seeing 11:11.

It seemed odd that the constant display of double numbers continued, even though the numbers displayed were different. There was a stirring inside my soul – a profound feeling that I was being guided to pay closer attention to certain moments in my life, whenever these numbers presented themselves. It was as though an inner silence swept through me every time the number sequences happened, begging me to look deeper, pay attention, and uncover something more that was surfacing in my awareness. The numbers were the trigger into that experience.

Six months later, the numbers 2:22 and 3:33 started to dissolve from my awareness and I started to encounter the numbers 4:44 and 5:55 everyday. What remained constant was I continued to experience deeper, more spiritual insights during times when those numbers presented themselves. Once I realized that seeing the double sets of numbers was stirring a deeper awareness in my consciousness, the numbers 5:55 became my predominant experience.

I began to experience 5:55 after I had the merging experience with my higher self and once I made the decision to live in my truth as opposed to following the inner critique. I was waking up to the truth of who I was and I could feel this happening deep within my soul. The regular display of numbers was like receiving breadcrumbs from my higher consciousness, serving the purpose of reflection – so I could take notice of the various degrees in my ascension.

11:11 occurred during a time when I was just beginning to wake up to the fact that signs and synchronicities are the purest way for the universe to express its love and wisdom to me. 5:55 appeared to me only after I obtained a new level of awareness – after I became more open and accepting of my higher self, and that other intelligences from higher realms were making regular contact with me.

The synchronistic events did not begin and end with numbers. The numbers were simply the means to get me to pay closer attention to the unspoken language of love.

How Synchronicities And Signs Reconnect Us To Love

Once I started to realize that the universe was 'talking to me' through the use of symbols and synchronicities, I discovered many other ways the universe was helping me learn to listen and pay attention. The various ways I was being communicated with were becoming more recognizable, more direct, and more apparent.

Every time I asked questions, no matter how complex, I was quickly provided with the answers. Sometimes the answers came through my dream state or through spirit guides. Other times, the answers came through another person. I also received answers by simply deepening the way I observed my surroundings; during the moment I was asking the question. To fully illustrate this, I will share this story:

One rainy evening, I tucked myself under an umbrella and went for a casual walk alone. I welcomed the sound and smell of rain as I found myself in a reflective, meditative state of consciousness. I felt safe and comfortable. There was little noise other than the splatter of raindrops bouncing off my umbrella and there were no people to distract me from contemplation.

Whenever I enter into this altered state of consciousness, I am alone with my thoughts, but I don't feel alone, because I sense a deeper connection to the entire universe. I know the universe knows I am there and is listening. With an open heart and mind, I ask life's biggest questions during these quiet, still moments, and the answers always seem to find me.

On that particular night, I asked my spirit guide, Melody, a question. As always, she answered me in loving reassurance, as I heard her voice telepathically travel through the void of my mind. I am filled with profound, awe-inspiring wonder, every time I have communication with Melody. She provides clarity from a spiritual perspective, helping me see beyond the physical point of view.

As I strolled along, I told Melody that I felt sad, because I wasn't able to help a family member who recently passed away at the age of 59. He died from heart disease, which was linked to a lifetime of unhealthy eating habits, a sedentary lifestyle, and emotional eating. I asked if there was something I could have done differently? Perhaps I could have shared some of the writings in my book that were still being written at that time, and perhaps this could have encouraged him to love himself more fully. Maybe I could have helped him live a longer life.

Melody replied, "Every person will always follow the path of least resistance. Habits become part of daily living and this keeps becoming reinforced, because those ideas and beliefs are rooted in older ideas and beliefs that people hold onto from the past. For example, if someone grows up feeling unworthy as a child, they will often take this belief into adulthood and they may continue to feel unworthy throughout life – making choices that continue to redefine the image they have about themselves, which is feeling unworthy."

As I was taking in this information, I stopped for a moment, because I became distracted by a large night crawler that was squirming on the sidewalk in front of me. I took a long look at the earthworm, because I knew there was a reason why I was drawn to it in that moment.

As I watched it wiggle and stretch, it seemed to have no idea where it was going. It squirmed into the cracks of the sidewalk and when the crack in the sidewalk contained too much water, the earthworm reversed its path and began squirming in the opposite direction.

I discovered something I had never noticed before; an earthworm can travel in either direction without having to turn around. There was no differentiation between moving forward or moving backwards. The worm was simply traveling the path of least resistance.

Everything Melody told me was validated in that moment. The answer to my question was mirrored in the form of a synchronistic event.

When we learn to tune into our surroundings, we will find that the universe is in synch with our consciousness – and that the answers to our questions are already there in our present state of awareness. All we need to do is explore our current surroundings a little more deeply, seek the answer that is in the moment of "now", because the universe is in constant communication with us.

Life is less complicated and mysterious when we rely on nature or our surroundings to guide us along our way. There are solutions to every problem, answers to every question, and love exists at every corner. The key is to remain open to all the ways that language is spoken and messages are delivered.

Receiving spiritual wisdom and information in this way is nothing new. Native Americans also accessed animal consciousness and nature's teachings to expand their own consciousness. They did this the same way – by asking a question, and turning to nature, people, and the journey itself to uncover the answers. It is just a matter of tuning into the frequency of All That Is. The only requirement is to be willing to want to know and learn more, and be open to all the ways that information can be received.

Physical reality is always whatever we perceive it to be, so I could have just as easily stumbled over the worm and learned nothing from it. I could have continued to stew in guilt and sadness that I was not better able to help the man who died. However, by knowing that the universe already holds the answers to life's greatest questions, and by taking a proactive approach to uncover what I desired to know, I discovered that the answers were right in front of me.

The key to connecting to the greater universal consciousness is to release any expectations about how you think you should receive information. Answers can come in an infinite number of ways. We only need to stay open and willing to tap into this greater knowledge base, and we will find that the universe is in constant communication with us. The more aware we are of all the ways we can uncover information, the more information we can extract from the universe.

This experience allowed me to let go of the guilt that stemmed from my belief that I was not able to do more. Traveling the path of least resistance is what we all do, because it is comfortable and it allows us to experience life to the best of our abilities. If we fall into destructive habits, because we carry a harmful set of beliefs along our journey, then we can thank the universe for showing us the path of least resistance, because it is along that path where we will find the most comfort. This is essential so that we can continue to proceed on our journey, while finding the greatest comfort, joy, and security along the way.

Synchronicities And Signs In Physical Reality

In another incident, synchronicities and signs showed a clear message when my eighty-seven-year-old aunt was admitted to the hospital. My aunt was experiencing severe chest pains after having undergone coronary bypass surgery three years prior. It appeared that her heart was beginning to fail.

My aunt never before experienced chest pains of this magnitude, not even prior to her bypass surgery, so we all felt that something was terribly wrong. My mother stayed by her side, while my aunt was prescribed morphine and bed-rest and we awaited her angiogram the next morning.

During this stressful waiting period, I asked my guide, Melody, if everything was going to be all right with my aunt. I received feedback from Melody that my aunt was going to be just fine and this was nothing serious. I had some doubt over what Melody was telling me, because my aunt continued to suffer with chest pains and the hospital staff was taking her condition seriously.

That evening, my mother came over for dinner. We each drank a glass of wine from two antique crystal glasses that my aunt gave me several years ago. These glasses are extremely delicate, engraved with fine etchings, and they are more than 100 years old. I normally don't drink out of them unless it's for a special occasion, and I'm not sure why I served wine from them on that particular evening.

The next morning, I asked my son to load the dishwasher. I forgot that I left the antique wine glasses next to the kitchen sink from the night before. I intended to wash them by hand that evening and safely put them away, but somehow I became distracted and forgot about them.

Meanwhile, my son loaded them into an over-filled dishwasher and also stacked heavy bowls on top of the glasses. He then proceeded to start the dishwasher. The dishwasher ran its full cycle and I remained oblivious to all of this.

Normally my husband volunteers to wash the dishes and unload the dishwasher, so the way these events unfolded was not usual and customary. Later that morning, I opened the dishwasher to unload it. I was shocked to see the stems of the wine glasses sticking out beneath heavy bowls that my son nonchalantly buried over the glasses.

A sick feeling welled up in my stomach. I was certain that once I removed the bowls from on top of the wine glasses, there would be cracks, gashes, and shards of glass below. I knew those thin, frail, wine glasses, could not have sustained this.

Upon lifting the bowls, I found both wine glasses were in perfect condition. There were no scratches, breaks, chips, and no damage at all.

Something pierced through my heart in that moment, and I knew I was having a physical experience that coincided with what Melody had already told me: My Aunt was going to be okay and she would survive whatever health condition she was going through. Although I was shrouded in doubt the day before, this incident touched me at the heart-level.

Later that afternoon, my mother called to give me the results of my aunt's angiogram. The doctors found no blockages. They contributed her chest pain to be from muscular problems stemming from her neck, from anxiety, or from other factors, because her angiogram did not show any anomalies whatsoever. She was released from the hospital the very next day.

How To Sharpen The Ability To Listen

I am thankful for the clairaudient relationship I have with my guides, who I call Melody, Baariq and The Voice of Creation. This book would not have come into existence, in the way it was written, without them. My state of consciousness, my willingness to be open, and quieting the ego mind, are the necessary prerequisites for being able to receive information from these highly evolved beings.

All of us receive guidance everyday. You may or may not be aware of the relationship you have with your own spirit guides, but your awareness of their presence has no bearing on their presence in your life. They are here assisting you, whether you are conscious of them or not.

We live in a highly intelligent universe and we are always connected to a universal mind. We can all access this higher mind, which holds a universal database of information and wisdom that benevolent extraterrestrials, angels, and spirit guides are also connected to.

As human beings, we have access to this same super-intelligence. When we listen from within instead of without, when we listen with our heart instead of our mind, and when we allow our imagination and inspirations to guide us, we will be accessing a higher intelligence from this higher mind.

The Language Of Love Is The Universal Language

We are fractals within a universe that is in constant communication with us and with itself. The language that the universe speaks is called love. This language of love is an energetic frequency, or a vibration, and we are giving this vibration a voice in everything we do and say.

The 'voice of love' is synonymous with the 'voice of creation', because the two are inseparable. You cannot have creation if there is no love or passion behind what you are creating and you cannot have love without the existence of creation. Therefore, you are love, and love is you. You can never be separate from this, because you exist within the body of creation.

The frequency of love is always part of who you are and you are constantly expressing love whether you are conscious of it or not. You are expressing love even when you are angry, depressed, or tired. You are an energetic being made from love, so anything and everything that comes from you is carrying this same frequency that you were created from.

The only reason we don't always see the expressions of love in everything we do and in every single experience is because we have simply moved out of our heart-space and we have aligned with our critical ego instead. The moment we choose to move back into our heart, we will see and experience love again.

Each one of us holds the blueprint for love. We all carry this within our unique signature so we can give love its infinite expression. This is why there are an infinite number of ways that love can be felt, perceived, transmitted, transformed and experienced. We are co-creators of love, because we turn this energetic frequency into something that can be experienced.

We find meanings for love, place value on love, give love its power, and find numerous ways to express, give, and feel love throughout our lives. Love is in everything, because it is everything. Love is not something that is earned and it is not something that we have to work for. Love simply is, all by itself. Love is the invisible thread, connecting the entire universe to itself, so that the universe can remain in constant communication with itself.

Love is "The Link", that humanity became unconscious of for a period of time. It is not that we became unconscious of love itself. We forgot that we are co-creators and transmitters for this energetic frequency and when we tap into it, there isn't anything we cannot be, do, or experience. The Voice of Creation provided "The 7 Principles of I AM", so we could all remember the truth about the magnificence of who we are and all that we are capable of.

You can hear The Voice of Creation whenever your heart is open to give and receive love. When your heart is open to this vibratory field, you can hear, see, and sense how love is being communicated through everything. The vibration of love is where creative solutions abound, where healing takes place, where genius, awe, and wonder exist, and this energetic field is always connected to you.

The physical world serves as a mirror, crystalizing energy into form so that energy can be experienced and played with in various ways and through different means. The physical world reflects the same vibration that is a match to your consciousness. When you think and see with your heart as opposed to listening to whatever is going on in your head, the physical world will reflect back a deeper wisdom that matches the vibration of love.

Your higher self, spirit guides, ascended masters, nature, and any deep human connections, are only able to connect to you through your heart. In order to experience this greater level of wisdom and understanding, it is important to remain heart centered and avoid siding with negative self-talk or negative emotions.

When you welcome negative thoughts or choose negative feelings, then this disconnects you from your heart. To shift back into heart centered thinking, simply think about the wonders of nature. Think about a new baby being born or how you feel when you play with a puppy. Invite ideas and thoughts into your mind that bring you joy and excitement and only focus on those. By shifting your thoughts to pure love and joy, you will immediately be back into your heart space, where infinite power, wisdom, and creativity abound.

When you want to give creation a voice in your own life, it does not matter how you do this. It does not matter who or what delivers love and wisdom to you. You and others will always benefit when the energetic expression is positive. All things positive, loving, joyful, and open, come from The Voice of Creation.

Whenever you choose to perceive a situation as infinite, positive, expansive, and joyful, you are tapping into the frequency of love, which is the frequency that exists in all of creation. When you choose to see every experience and every person in the most positive light, you will automatically connect to your heart-space. This is where you will find your link to a universal source of energy. This is where you will discover your own magnificence, the genius within, your ability to heal, experience a heightened level of energy, personal power, and where you can tap into infinite knowledge, wisdom, and joy.

We are fractals of creation and we are always connected to this frequency. This means that the answers already exist within the one asking the questions. The ability to heal from any illness already exists within you. The ability to find a solution to every perceived problem already exists before you. Infinite wisdom can be delivered to you in an infinite number of ways, which is always at your disposal. It is up to you, the seeker, to tune your heart to this frequency that you already inhabit, so it can be made manifest through you.

Artists, musicians, actors, dancers, and writers, find that when they open their heart and quiet their critical, analytical mind, their greatest work comes through. When you connect energetically with love, instead of physically through the ego mind, you become one with something greater than the physical self. You become a channel, who is capable of absorbing information from the same field where there is creative genius. There are no limits or shortages of this overflowing, abundant energy that you are connected to.

This is where you will discover multidimensional aspects of yourself, including the channel to your higher self. To have a life of "more" instead of a life of "less" comes from desiring it and believing it is possible, which is a feeling that comes from the heart. What you feel in your heart is what connects you to this infinite field of universal energy. Simply trust and welcome all the goodness that comes your way without judgment or discernment.

When you are judgmental (judge mental) about the process, you are literally inviting the mental mind into your consciousness, or the ego mind to judge you. You cannot be in your heart-center if you are choosing to be in a state of judgment.

If you doubt or stop the process and remove yourself from operating out of pure bliss and joy because you tell yourself that you can't channel more advanced information, that you are not connected to All That Is, or if you tell yourself that this is nonsense, you will break the connection. The universe isn't going to argue with you or attempt to persuade you to believe anything other than what you choose to believe. This is a free will universe. If you believe in limitation, then this will be your manifestation.

In the moments that you want to receive answers to your questions, allow yourself to be like the child you once were, where there were no judgments and no restrictions within your imagination.

You are free to be the real you and you don't have to host any critical beliefs about yourself. You are free to love yourself as fully as you can. You can own every moment that you are alive and choose to live your life in the highest frequency of love that you can imagine.

Each moment is always YOUR moment to do as you please. Whatever comes to you will provide you with everything you need in your moment. Why not take this moment to lift yourself up? Allow the vibration of love to carry you to a place where you feel infinitely joyous, loved, and supported.

Remember that you are not the story of your life, but rather, you are the experiencer of a story that has been scripted by you. When you see your life in this way, you will find that it is not necessary to take physical reality so seriously, and you don't have to react to everything. Instead, you can view the people and experiences in your life as "tools" that serve the purpose of helping you grow spiritually.

When you know you are having a physical existence so you can grow spiritually, you can reach into your toolbox and ask yourself, "What could this next tool be used for?" When you look, listen, and ask the universe for the lessons in every experience, you will start to notice the lessons.

Physical reality is a mirror, always reflecting and always providing exactly what you need. Simply take a look in the mirror and trust whatever you are being shown. Physical reality is your tool for ascension.

Make Your Life's Journey A Joyful One

The greatest journey you can travel already exists within you. Decide to bring your wildest dreams into fruition by allowing yourself to be filled with the greatest joy and passion that you can possibly imagine for yourself. You will find you can always take it to the next highest level when you do this. This is because creation is infinite. You are the only one who sets limits. If you want to experience more oneness and peace, you can have this right now. If you want to experience a more loving relationship with your partner, you can bring that forth right now. If you want to experience more abundance in your life, all you need to do is notice the abundance all around you.

Allow yourself to experience joy as if it were a cup that keeps running over. You can experience the most intense feelings of joy by simply imagining it. Then, after you have imagined it, challenge yourself to imagine your present level of joy to be even greater than the last moment. Keep doing this until a joyful feeling runs over the top.

Anytime you live according to your highest excitement, follow your bliss, and travel the path of least resistance, you will discover your highest truth of who you are. You will be living totally in alignment with your higher self. You don't ever need to set limits on how much joy you want to experience. You also don't need to set limits on how much wisdom you want to obtain, or how much love you want to experience.

The nature of creation is that it is infinite and limitless. Allow yourself to be all that you have been created to be, which is someone with unlimited potential.

This is the way the higher self operates. It will keep recreating itself as a being with unlimited potential, because this is the very nature of creation. It is infinite, open, and expansive. This is your true nature. When you take joy to a level that feels infinite, you are simultaneously lifting the blocks and limitations of the ego and you are opening your heart, which connects you to the highest vibration of love. When you allow love and joy to come through your heart in every moment, you are opening the doorway to your higher self. You are ascending.

There are times when you won't feel connected to your higher self, and there are times when you will feel depressed and disconnected. This is normal, because more than one aspect of you exists. You are a multidimensional being.

There are times when you will need to experience isolation, selfishness, sadness, separation, and anger, in order to figure out how to manifest what you prefer. These experiences serve a greater purpose. Uncomfortable feelings and pain teach us to notice our perceived limitations so we can take a closer look at beliefs that no longer serve us.

Pain prompts us to ask questions and look to the source of our pain so we can begin to heal. When the pain becomes too great to continue down the path we have been on, nature will hold our hand while we travel a new path of least resistance.

When we invite change into our lives, a new road will stretch out before us – one that would not have been discovered if the road we grew used to did not become rough and bumpy. Pain leads to change, and change creates spiritual evolution and growth.

Every emotion you feel comes from some sort of belief you have chosen to hang onto and identify with. When you change what you think is true about yourself to be positive and expansive, you will experience accompanying emotions that are joyful, loving, and peaceful.

Your mood is always a reflection of underlying beliefs. When you change your beliefs about what you think is true, your mood will shift to be in alignment with what you believe.

Your higher self does not reside in the same plane where there is self-criticism, self-loathing, or where there is anger and resentment. The higher self is directly linked to the vibration of love and the "I AM" in creation, so when you decide to fill your mind with limited negative beliefs that fuel negative emotions, you are simultaneously blocking your higher self from being the director in your life.

Which aspect of YOU do you want to BE? There are many

versions of yourself that you can BE in any moment. You cannot consciously experience all of your selves at once, but you can choose to experience the self that is most reflective of your highest and greatest good, which is simultaneously providing the greatest benefits to humanity.

If you can imagine a happier you, then that version of YOU already exists. Grab onto that "you" and claim ownership of it. It belongs to you and you can allow that self to be the "you" that you already are.

It is always up to you to decide to BE the person you wish to come into and be-come. Why not choose to align your consciousness with the higher, loving, nonjudgmental aspect of yourself right now? You are the only ONE in this entire universe that has the power to claim YOUR vibrational frequency. This makes YOU the most powerful person in the universe.

You ARE The I AM

You have been provided with a greater awareness of yourself through the principles in this book. You have been shown that you are more than just a physical body, and that you are an infinite being, having a multidimensional existence, because you are pure conscious energy. You have been shown that your ego's construct of separatism is an illusion and this is the only thing that prevents you from living as your true self. You have been shown how you co-create your reality, whether you are conscious of this or not. You know that you are a being of love who has been wired for love.

When you meditate on "The 7 Principles of I AM", it will become clear that there is no difference between you and the one who created you. You exist within the body of creation as a product of these seven principles. YOU ARE the I AM.

It may be helpful to write the seven principles on a piece of paper and carry them with you for a while, reflecting on them as you go about your day. When you are conscious that these principles are the true nature of who you are, this will align you with your higher self, which will bring more peace, joy, and love into your life.

1. I AM Pure Conscious Energy

2. I AM Whole. I AM ONE

3. I AM Not The Ego

4. I AM Multidimensional

5. I AM Timeless, Infinite, and Eternal

6. I AM Creative and Expansive

7. I AM Love

QUESTIONS & ANSWERS

Where did "The 7 Principles of I AM" come from?

"The 7 Principles of I AM" were literally given to me one night while I was asleep. A voice woke me up and asked me to write down seven principles as they were spoken to me. I did not know what this was about at the time. I didn't have time to think. I simply wrote what I heard and the thinking came later.

As I started to reflect on my own experiences, I researched and gathered information to support the concepts that were relayed to me, and that is how my writing journey began. This same voice continued to come through intermittently, as I began writing this book, especially in the introductory section where each principle is defined.

The voice never referred to itself by name, so I decided to call it "The Voice of Creation" in order to differentiate what I heard coming through, as opposed to what I had to think about and research on my own. There is a different flow and conciseness in the energy and intelligence when channeling. I can't take full credit for the entire body of this work and I shouldn't pretend to. I am just an ordinary person who happens to be able to hear or tap into another frequency or other dimensions where other worldly beings exist.

I became the student of my own work, learning and digesting the principles as I was writing about them. The information transformed my life more than anything else I have ever come across. Whenever I shared my experiences and the techniques I was learning with other people, I began to notice great transformation in other people's lives as well.

I received a lot of support while this book was in the works, not only from friends and family, but also in the way of experiencing an insurmountable number of synchronicities, along with regular visitations, and spiritual breakthroughs, which provided me with the confirmation I needed to be able to move forward and reduce self-doubt.

Why were you chosen to be an emissary for this information?

I have been told by the beings who communicate with me that I am one of them. Although I do not have any memory of being born anywhere else other than on this planet, I do have memories of having several past lives or past incarnations where I was a less evolved spiritually.

During this lifetime, I have received several vibrational upgrades by the beings who regularly visit me. This was necessary so I could receive the higher vibrational frequencies transmitting from these higher realms. This allowed me to be able to perceive and relay the information they were giving me.

Eventually, I was able to integrate and merge with my higher self, whom I know is a fifth dimensional being. I also remember making a promise that I would be of service to humanity no matter what, and I was not going to leave this planet until my work was complete. I was well aware of this from the time I was a child. I also always knew my life's work would involve writing or authoring a book, but the details were not clear until only a few years ago.

Do you think full disclosure or extraterrestrial contact with all of humanity is in our future?

Yes, I do think that eventually, everyone will be ready for contact, but for now, these beings are not going to suddenly land on the white house lawn. They honor our free will and the majority of humanity is not ready for this level of contact yet.

Instead, the information they are sharing about the operations of the universe, how consciousness evolves, and the nature of our soul, is being channeled through human emissaries, like myself.

THE LINK – QUESTIONS & ANSWERS

I serve as a receiver and a communicator for this information to come through for those who are ready to receive it and integrate it into their lives. Our free will is always honored. Each one of us is not going to be given more than we can digest, nor are we able to perceive what we are not the vibration of. It is always our choice to take what resonates and discard what doesn't.

As humanity becomes more evolved collectively in consciousness, more of this information will filter to the masses. For now, the information presented in this book is meant to help fill in the blanks where spiritual teachers from the past left off, or where ancient wisdoms was lost, and it will provide a stepping stone for more information to come from other emissaries in the future. This information is not new nor am I the first person who has been contacted to deliver this type of information. This information is the same truth that originated from our ancestors thousands of years ago, before it became lost knowledge. This information is simply being brought to the surface again to help us remember who we truly are.

Do you have any insights about the future of humanity?

There is no doubt that humanity has been on a path of destruction and we will continue along this same path, if we don't change our ways. No one is going to rescue us from the choices we are making in our daily lives; however, we can learn new skills and discover new ways of thinking that will align us towards the path of ascension. We can remember the ancient wisdom we have lost.

It's important to realize that the destructive patterns and consequences of our choices are not our fault. This is the result of losing our awareness of our true origin of oneness. Once we begin to relearn and remember what we have forgotten, humanity will shift in consciousness and there will be an end to all the destruction.

With an end to destruction, there will also be an end to ignorance, greed, poverty, inequality, and to all things that keep us separate. The illusion of separation has kept us from evolving and expanding in our consciousness.

The only way that more evolved beings can help us is that we must be open and willing to learn and embrace the teachings they are here to deliver. Nothing is going to be shoved down our throat and forced upon us. We have free will and it is up to us to take hold of the information and integrate it into our lives. It is up to us to heal the wounds within ourselves before any wounds can heal in the outside world. We have been given the tools, and humanity must decide what will be done with these tools.

How can I apply "The 7 Principles of I AM" in my own life?

Working with "The 7 Principles of I AM" is not something that anyone can do in an instant. The content in this book is intense and concentrated, and it is best absorbed when it's read several times, and when you integrate these principles in your own meditation and into your everyday circumstances.

If you feel that something resonates from this book, allow yourself to take it as far as you can. Think about your own experiences and the synchronicities in your life and how these principles apply to you.

Don't worry if you still have issues with the ego mind, or if you still resort to programmed responses like anger or fear, or if you still have trouble understanding that you are a multidimensional being. All of this will become clearer over time. Transformation is about learning new skills and letting go of old programs, which cannot happen in an instant.

Celebrate every new discovery and rejoice in every little step that leads to more joy and more love in your life. If you experience even a little more joy and love in your life than you felt before, then treat this as a milestone. There will be more experiences like this when you choose to keep integrating this type of information into your life and by intending to make ascension a part of your life experience.

There will also be sequels to this book, webinars, workbooks, and other resources to help you with more hands-on methods for integrating "The 7 Principles of I AM" in your life.

Visit: www.LinkToTheLink.com for the latest updates.

GLOSSARY

ascension: The act of moving to a higher dimension, spirituality through the raising of one's vibrational frequency. Living in more light body that is less dense, and awaking to an expansion in one's consciousness which may include becoming more psychic, joyful, loving, and unified with oneself and others.

chakra: A vortex or gateway that spins allowing the flow of universal energy to come in and go out, linking the spiritual to the physical.

consciousness: Your ability to observe, perceives, and experience your reality. Your consciousness is the state of your soul.

double slit experiment: This experiment provides evidence at the quantum level that everything begins as a wave, but the act of observation transforms waves of energy into particles of matter.

clairaudience: The ability to hear sound telepathically, without the aid of physical ears.

clairvoyance: The inner sense of sight without the aid of physical eyes. The third eye is said to be the method for seeing clairvoyantly with the mind's eye.

dimensions: Levels of awareness in consciousness, with varying degrees of frequencies. Higher dimensions are experienced as divine, etheric, or spiritual; and lower dimensions are experienced as being denser, material, and physical.

enlightenment: The illumination that occurs when one awakens more fully, recognizing the true nature of oneself.

fractal: A fragmented geometric shape that can be subdivided into parts, each of which is reduced-size copy of the whole.

frequency: The rate or number of waves that pass through a specific point in a certain period of time, constituting a vibration.

holographic universe: The understanding that the universe is holographic in nature, in which the micro is an exact replica of the macro, and the entire universe is reflected within every point in the cosmos.

left brain: The left hemisphere of the brain is characterized by logical thought processes, understanding sequences, placing ideas into categories, and understanding parts of the whole. The left brain is also where the negative ego or the inner critique resides.

Mandelbrot set: A set of complex numbers that creates a infinite repetition of the same pattern, also found in nature such as plant parts, coastal and mountain ranges, river branches, lightening, and in clouds.

parallel universe: A theory of a self-contained separate reality co-existing with one's own. A specific group of parallel universes is called a multiverse.

right brain: The right hemisphere of the brain is characterized by creative thought processes. It recognizes patterns and synchronicities, and the unification of all things. The right brain links the heart to the higher mind, forming a triad for expanded awareness and communication.

SOURCES

Author's Preface

1. Kevin D. Randle and Donald R. Schmitt, UFO Crash at Roswell (New York: Avon Books 1991).
2. Stanton Friedman and Kathleen Marden, *Captured! The Betty and Barney Hill UFO Experience: The True Story of the World's First Documented Alien Abduction* (New Jersey: The Career Press 2007).
3. Travis Walton, *Fire In The Sky* (New York: Marlowe & Company 1997).
4. Linda Moulton Howe, *Glimpses of Other Realities: Volume II: High Strangeness* (Pennsylvania: LMH Productions, 1998).

Chapter One

5. Space.com: Elusive Dark Energy Is Real, Study Says. Posted September 12, 2012. http://www.space.com/17549-dark-energy-real-universe-expansion.html (visited 6-15-2014)
6. The Healer's Journal. The 7 Quantum Physics Theories That Explain How Everything is Made of Energy. Posted May 5, 2013. http://www.thehealersjournal.com/2013/05/05/quantum-physics-explain-how-everything-is-made-of-energy/#sthash.6WCjWkmo.dpuf (visited 6-17-2014)
7. The Double Slit Experiment. http://doubleslitexperiment.com (visited 6-28-2014)
8. Image taken from: The Artificial Human. Jason Gregory. (Accessed 7-2-2014)
9. The Telegraph. Pictures of the year 2010: space - Hubble, Chandra and Spitzer telescope images http://www.telegraph.co.uk/news/picturegalleries/pictures-of-the-year/8199414/Pictures-of-the-year-2010-space-Hubble-Chandra-and-Spitzer-telescope-images.html?image=21 (visited 7-30-2014)
10. Image of Nerve Cell. http://fotoneuron.narod.ru/pictures /2_6.jpg (visited 7-30-2014)
11. 10 Fascinating People With Savant Syndrome. By Andrew Handly. July 23, 2013. http://listverse.com/2013/07/23/10-

fascinating-people-with-savant-syndrome (visited 9-21-2015)

12. Derek Amato Becomes Musical Genius After Brain Injury: What Is Acquired Savant Syndrome? By Nadia-Elysse Harris. October 19, 2013. http://www.medicaldaily.com/derek-amato-becomes-musical-genius-after-brain-injury-what-acquired-savant-syndrome-video-260369 (visited 10-12-2015)

13. Amnesiac Man Wakes Up From Coma Speaking Only Ancient Hebrew. By Barbara Johnson. September 10, 2015. http://worldnewsdailyreport.com/amnesiac-man-wakes-from-coma-speaking-only-ancient-hebrew/ (visited 10-12-2015)

14. The 5 Strangest Cases of Simultaneous Invention. By Chris Bucholz. February 8, 2013. http://www.cracked.com/blog/the-5-strangest-cases-simultaneous-invention/ (visited 3-6-2014)

15. Rupert Sheldrake. The Extended Min: Recent Experimental Evidence. Google Tech Talk September 2, 2008. http://www.sheldrake.org/videos/the-extended-mind-recent-experimental-evidence (visited 3-9-2014)

16. Burpo, Todd, and Lynn Vincent. Heaven is for Real: A Little Boy's Astounding Story of His Trip to Heaven and Back. (Nashville: Thomas Nelson, Inc., 2010).

17. "Is Consciousness Produced by the Brain?" By Bruce Greyson https://www.youtube.com/watch?v=sPGZSC8odIU (visited 3-29-2014)

18. The New York Times Magazine: Cleve Backster. By Josh Eells. http://www.nytimes.com/news/the-lives-they-lived/2013/12/21/cleve-backster/ (visited 4-5-2014)

19. Wikipedia. The Free Encyclopedia. Prana https://en.wikipedia.org/wiki/Prana (visited 4-17-2014)

20. [Discover Your Awakening]. Image Retrieved from: http://discoveryourawakening.com/blog (visited 4-12-2014)

21. METAtonin Research - The Pineal Gland and the Chemistry of Consciousness http://metatoninresearch.org/ (visited 7-8-2014)

22. The Pineal Gland: A Neuroendocrine Transducer of Light Information. By Anamika Sengupta and Gianluca Tosini. July 11, 2011. http://www.photobiology.info/Tosini.html (visited 7-8-2014)

23. Project SCANATE - The Roots Of Stargate. By Michael Jura http://blog.learnremoteviewing.com/?p=1560 (visited 8-15-2014)

Chapter Two

24. PBS Nova; Cut to the Heart. Amazing Heart Factshttp://www.pbs.org/wgbh/nova/heart/heartfacts.html.
25. Image taken from: PBS Nova; A Radical Mind. October 1, 2008. http://www.pbs.org/wgbh/nova/physics/mandelbrot-fractal.html (visited 9-9-2014)
26. Image taken from: Time Lightbox; Finding Beauty: Fractal Patterns on Earth as Seen from Space.
By, Vaughn Wallace. September 19, 2012 http://lightbox.time.com/2012/09/19/finding-beauty-fractal-patterns-on-earth-as-seen-from-space (visited 9-18-2014)
27. Image taken from: Vizproto Website. http://vizproto.wikispaces.asu.edu/DakGid (visited 9-19-2014)
28. Encyclopedia Britannica: Leonardo Pisano. By, Frances Carney Gies.
http://www.britannica.com/EBchecked/topic/336467/Leonardo-Pisano (visited 9-20-2014)
29. University of Minnesota Science and Technology Center. The Geometry Center: The Golden Ratio.
http://www.geom.uiuc.edu/~demo5337/s97b/art.htm (visited 10-1-2014)
30. The Human Body and the Golden Ratio. By, Gary Meisner. May 31, 2012. http://www.goldennumber.net/human-body (visited 10-1-2014)
31. Quantum "spooky action at a distance" travels at least 10,000 times faster than light. By, Brian Dodson. March 10, 2013 http://www.gizmag.com/quantum-entanglement-speed-10000-faster-light/26587 (visited 10-11-2014)
32. Wikipedia. No Child Left Behind Act of 2001. (NCLB) http://en.wikipedia.org/wiki/No_Child_Left_Behind_Act (visited 11-2-2014)
33. Pittsburg Post-Gazette. No Child Left Behind has altered the face

of education. By, Joe Smydo. August 28, 2006
http://www.post-gazette.com/news/education/2006/08/28/No-Child-Left-Behind-has-altered-the-face-of-education/stories/200608280126 (visited 11-6-2014)
34. Huffington Post Education. No Child Left Behind Worsened Education, 48 Percent of Americans 'Very Familiar' With The Law Say In Gallup Poll. August 21, 2012.
http://www.huffingtonpost.com/2012/08/21/no-child-left-behind-wors_n_1819877.html (visited 11-6-2014)
35.) http://www.bloomberg.com/news/articles/2014-05-07/student-loan-interest-rates-rise-for-2014-2015-school-year By, Janet Lorin. May 7, 2014. (visited 11-9-2014)
36. Board of the Governors of the Federal Reserve. Who Owns the Federal Reserve?
http://www.federalreserve.gov/faqs/about_14986.htm (visited 11-11-2014)
37. Who Owns The Federal Reserve? By Ellen Brown. February 8 2014. http://globalresearch.ca/who-owns-the-federal-reserve/10489 (visited 11-11-2014)
38. PBS News Hour. Greenspan Examines Federal Reserve, Mortgage Crunch. September 18, 2007.
http://www.pbs.org/newshour/bb/business-july-dec07-greenspan_09-18/ (visited 11-13-2014)
39. John F. Kennedy vs The Federal Reserve
http://john-f-kennedy.net/thefederalreserve.htm (visited 11-14-2014)

Chapter Three

40. McCraty, Rollin, Mike Atkinson, and Dana Tomasino. Heartmath Research Center: Science Of The Heart. Exploring The Role Of The Heart In Human Performance. Publication Number: 01-001. Boulder City, California: HeartMath Research Center, 2001. Web. 11 Oct 2015.
https://www.heartmath.org/assets/uploads/2015/01/science-of-the-heart.pdf (visited 1-17-2015)

41. HeartMath Institute. An Appreciative Heart Is Good Medicine. July 2, 2009. https://www.heartmath.org/articles-of-the-heart/personal-development/an-appreciative-heart-is-good-medicine (visited 1-17-2015)

42. The Heart Has Its Own 'Brain' and Consciousness. By Rollin McCraty, Ph.D., Raymond Trevor Bradley, Ph.D. and Dana Tomasino, BA. January 10, 2015. http://in5d.com/the-heart-has-its-own-brain-and-consciousness (visited 1-22-2015)

43. Heart Mastery. Heart Facts. http://heartmastery.com/about-us/heart-facts (visited 2-5-2015)

44. American Society of Clinical Oncology. One in Three People with Cancer Has Anxiety or Other Mental Health Challenges. By Kate Blackburn. October 6, 2014. http://www.asco.org/press-center/one-three-people-cancer-has-anxiety-or-other-mental-health-challenges (visited 2-10-2015)

45. INTEGRIS. James L. Hall Jr. Center for Mind, Body and Spirit. Studies On Mind Body Connection. http://integrisok.com/mind-body-spirit/studies-on-mind-body-connection (visited 2-10-2015)

Chapter Four

46. Do Parallel Universes Really Exist? By Josh Clark http://science.howstuffworks (visited 3-3-2015)

47. Jill Bolte Taylor, My Stroke of Insight, A Brain Scientist's Personal Journey (New York: Penguin Group, 2006).

48. Wikipedia: Indigo children http://en.wikipedia.org/wiki/Indigo_children (visited 5-25-2015)

Chapter Five

49. How Stuff Works: Does Time Change Speed. By John Fuller. http://science.howstuffworks.com/science-vs-myth/everyday-myths/time-dilation1.htm (visited 3-5-2015)

50. Wikepedia: Yugi http://en.wikipedia.org/wiki/Yuga (visited 3-13-2015)

51. Image Taken From: American Institute of Vedic Studies. Secrets of the Yugas or World-Ages http://vedanet.com/2012/06/13/secrets-of-the-yugas-or-world-ages/ (Accessed 3-19-2015)
52. Mayan End Age 12-21-2012 Heralds a New Age of Spiritual Enlightenment http://www.adishakti.org/mayan_end_times_prophecy_12-21-2012.htm (visited 3-6-2015)
53. Ancient Egypt Reincarnation. By Globerover. March 29, 2010 http://globerove.com/egypt/ancient-egyptian-reincarnation/3229 (visited 2-10-2015)
54. 5 Reasons We May Live In A Multiverse. By Clara Moskowitz. December 7, 2012 http://www.space.com/18811-multiple-universes-5-theories.html (visited 3-30-2015)
55. The Web Of Life. By Taino Ti. September 2005 http://www.susunweed.com/herbal_ezine/September05/goddess.htm (visited 4-10-2015)
56. Indra's Net. Wikipedia. https://en.wikipedia.org/wiki/Indra%27s_net (visited 4-10-2015)

Chapter Six

57. The Story of Colonel Sanders, a Man who Started at 65 and Failed 1009 Times Before Succeeding. July 25, 2012. http://yourstory.com/2012/07/the-story-of-colonel-sanders-a-man-who-started-at-65-and-failed-1009-times-before-succeeding/ (visited 6-12-2015)
58. Success Story of KFC. http://greatsuccessstory.weebly.com/success-story-of-kfc.html (visited 6-12-2015)

ABOUT THE AUTHOR

Kendra Jonas is a business owner, author, public speaker, and holistic life coach. She received her Bachelor of Art's Degree in Sociology with a minor in Art from Portland State University and received a second Bachelor's Degree (BFA) in Digital Communications from American Intercontinental University, graduating Summa Cum Laude.

Kendra has achieved financial independence as an entrepreneur who founded several businesses, which have provided services geared to help others become more financially independent in their professional lives. In her book entitled, "The Link", Kendra reveals her journey involving regular communication with other worldly beings, which led to her breakthroughs in the expansion of her own consciousness.

"The Link" examines "The 7 Principles of I AM", which have helped countless people unleash their own untapped potential. This book provides unparalleled wisdom and a new set of tools for achieving fifth dimensional consciousness that takes us to the next level in spiritual awakening and ascension.